"This is a well-written, scholarly work that doesn't require a scholarly mind to read, enjoy, and become enlightened by! It's clear in its direction and purpose to 'present Christ in a different light' than our more fundamental Christian Brothers and Sisters currently are . . . This is a book for these current times in our Christian Churches and is well worth the read. I highly recommend it!"

—**KIM ROSSI**, St Stephan's Episcopal Church, Olean, New York

"*Onward Christian Soldiers?* is a book for . . . faithful, well-meaning believers [who] don't realize how completely American Civil Religion and fundamentalism have twisted and misrepresented Biblical truth in many of our churches and in the public square. In a scholarly, yet entertaining manner, Cheek exposes these distortions . . . Be prepared to be amused, offended, and challenged. But most of all, be prepared to see the world in a new way; a better way; a more God-pleasing way; and to have your fear replaced with joy and . . . love."

—**DANIEL BURINGRUD**, St. Paul's Family Church (ELCA), Ellicottville, New York

Onward Christian Soldiers?

Onward Christian Soldiers?

One Pastor's Journey from Fundamentalism to Discipleship

DEREK J. CHEEK

WIPF & STOCK · Eugene, Oregon

ONWARD CHRISTIAN SOLDIERS?
One Pastor's Journey from Fundamentalism to Discipleship

Wipf & Stock
An Imprint of Wipf and Stock Publishers
199 W. 8th Ave., Suite 3
Eugene, OR 97401

www.wipfandstock.com

PAPERBACK ISBN: 978-1-5326-4965-3
HARDCOVER ISBN: 978-1-5326-4966-0
EBOOK ISBN: 978-1-5326-4967-7

Manufactured in the U.S.A.   08/24/18

This book is dedicated to all who have been wounded
by congregations and ministers who have lead with
legalism and judgmentalism,
rather than the grace, mercy, and love of God seen in Jesus Christ.
Kyrie eleison!

Contents

Acknowledgements

Rev. Jerry leFeber, who has always been a mentor and soul friend;

Cohort brothers Rev. Dr. Mike Branscombe, Rev. Dr. Mike Philliber, and

Rev. Paul Rebelo, with whom I've spent untold hours honing my beliefs and practices . . . and there may have been some cigars and scotch, too!

Rev. Phil Esala, who stood at the beginning of my journey into the ministry and always pointed me to Jesus as the ground of all we do;

Mr. Tim Alexander, who suggested *many* vital editorial and thematic improvements;

Rev. Dan Buringrud, who read versions of this text and offered advice;

Mrs. Gert Yohe, Mrs. Roxane Struchen, and Mrs. Theresa Heinz, who have always pushed me to justify my thoughts with scriptural support and pastoral care;

Rev. Dr. Bruce Levine, whose thoughtfulness has made me think deeper;

Rev. Marie Meeks; the Very Rev. Fr. Greg Dobson, VF; Rev. Dan McDowell; Rev. Phil Houghton, Rev. LaMont Higgenbottom; Fr. Tony Salim, Rev. Kim Rossi, and Rev. Susan Block, clergy colleagues whose advice and friendship has always been unquestioned—may every minister have such companions!

This book was proofread and edited by Sue Zebrosky, her keen eye and diligent help have vastly improved it. *Thanks!*

Introduction

I thought the purpose of education
was to learn to think for yourself.

—JOHN KEATING IN *DEAD POET'S SOCIETY*[1]

He most lives who thinks most,
feels the noblest,
acts the best.

—PHILIP JAMES BAILEY[2]

CHRISTIANITY IS UNDER ASSAULT in the United States of America. But not so much by those whom we are frequently told are trying to destroy it: people who say "happy holidays" instead of a hearty "merry Christmas," or those who support LGBTQ equality, or even by those who are pro-choice. Christianity isn't being assailed by people who supposedly "hate" Christ[3] nearly so much as by those who call themselves his followers. It's being harmed far more by many of those who believe with every fiber of their beings that they are serving Jesus the most. It's beset by Christians whose Christianity is defined more by what (and who) they are *against* than what and whom they are *for*.

In this book I wish to present Christ in a different light from the Christianity of these brothers and sisters. And I'm inviting you to join me. I

1. *Dead Poet's Society* (film) directed by Peter Weir.
2. Bailey, *Festus*.
3. A group whose animus is far more manufactured than it is genuine.

1

want to state emphatically, here at the very outset, that I believe those from whom I am differentiating myself *are* Christians—my spiritual brothers and sisters. I believe they mean well. I respect that they are trying to obey God as they understand him. But I also believe that they have profoundly misunderstood him. The Christ they proclaim is a poor reflection of the Jesus we see in the Bible.

I desire to present Christ in ways that are more faithful to Jesus as we see him in Matthew, Mark, Luke and John. To do that I'm going to come clean: *theologically* I'm a "moderate," a "progressive," a "post-liberal," a "post-evangelical," or just a garden-variety "liberal." I wish to reclaim the *honor* in holding well-considered and tempered ideals about Christ-following at a time when so many seem to be running further and faster to a regressive version of Jesus nested in the "comfort" of an oversimplified and idealized past.

Many modern American Christians are on a vain quest, seeking to reconstruct idyllic days that were never as tranquil as they imagine (or "remember") . . . at least not for *everyone*. The "orthodoxy" they seek in the past was never as pure as they believe. Furthermore, modern scholarship has revealed data to which our forbearers had no access, and we are responsible to incorporate *that* knowledge into *our* discipleship. Rather than clawing our way backwards, or presenting Christianity in terms of what we're *against*, I believe followers of Christ should proclaim the positive things we see Jesus teaching: a theology rooted in sacrificial love and built by working to extend dignity and equality to all people.

Consider the words of the apostle Paul: "Be devoted to one another in love. Honor one another above yourselves."[4] And ponder the message of Pricilla:[5] "[L]et us consider how we may spur one another on toward love and good deeds, not giving up meeting together, as some are in the habit of doing."[6] Christianity is practiced best when it is *lived*. Far too many "Christians" have turned it into some sort of test of biblical "knowledge." James addresses this problem in his epistle: "What good is it, my brothers and sisters, if someone claims to have faith but has no deeds? Can such faith save them? Suppose a brother or a sister is without clothes and daily food. If one of you says to them, 'Go in peace; keep warm and well fed,' but does

---

4. Romans 12:10.

5. I believe Adolf von Harnack is correct that Priscilla is the author of Hebrews. Other possibilities include: Barnabas (Tertullian and Jerome), Apollos (Luther), or Silas.

6. Hebrews 10:24–25.

nothing about their physical needs, what good is it? In the same way, faith by itself, if it is not accompanied by action, is dead. But someone will say, 'You have faith; I have deeds.' Show me your faith without deeds, and I will show you my faith by my deeds."[7]

I'm painfully aware that writing as I am might seem to be a case of exactly what I'm suggesting we should *not* be doing! And that may be a fair criticism. I will say this in my defense: while I take issue with fundamentalism and evangelicalism, I am *not* taking personal issue with individual fundamentalists or evangelicals. I believe the people who embrace those systems of theology are my brothers and sisters in Christ—they're "saved," to use their terminology. I will offer critiques to some of *what* they believe, and some of the *ways* they live out their faith in Christ: what kind of "fruit" they are bearing.[8] I will base my critiques on Scripture, especially passages that feature the actions or clear teachings of our Lord, Jesus. My critique is purely theological, and in no way personal.

I hope this book is read by people who are members of fundamentalist and evangelical congregations. I especially hope that people who already have some misgivings about the theology of their "conservative" church home consider the thoughts expressed here. I want to normalize your experience and the fears you likely have in the back of your mind. I want you to know I *was* you. I have been there—really.

As I passed an early draft of this book to a couple colleagues, they suggested that I *own* my credentials as a full-fledged fundamentalist-turned-"Bible-denying-liberal."[9] I had not originally planned to do that. They suggested I can say things directly to the evangelical and fundamentalist branch of the church with an *authenticity* that most other "moderates" lack, because I *know* by personal experience (existentially) what is proclaimed from the pulpits of many fundamentalist churches and how it makes people feel. I spent over a decade hearing it firsthand. I was educated in their institutions. It was in their colleges and seminaries that I went rogue and became whatever it is I have become. And while it's true I'm a former-fundamentalist-turned-*something*, whatever I *have* become, it isn't

---

7. James 2:14–18.

8. Matthew 7:18–20.

9. At the risk of sounding snarky, I have claimed this moniker as a badge of honor. Some local clergy applied it to me years ago as we were discussing some of the topics that are presented here. It was intended as a bit of a joke, and I use it in that spirit.

Bible-denying. I would suggest that as I have learned to read the Bible *less* literally, I have come to understand it *more* profoundly.

I *was* raised to be a fundamentalist. I was given a nearly unassailable confidence that what I was taught was the *only* correct understanding of things. To stray from that "one true path" was to risk the eternal torments of hell—truly—or to at least risk being branded "unusable" for *God's work* in this life. Neither prospect was attractive. Except, in my case, something went wrong in my training. I began doubting the accuracy of many of the claims of my fundamentalist teachers. I wasn't convinced that *eternal death in hell* was the ultimate end of people who trusted in Christ, but questioned, for example, creation as the product of seven, *literal*, twenty-four-hour days. I could see the story of Genesis 1–3 as a *metaphor* for a God who created through an evolutionary process spanning billions of years. And the more I compared the science of both camps, the more convinced I became that "young Earth"[10] proponents were simply wrong. Which led me to more thoroughly investigate the position of Christian theologians who suggest the Genesis creation account was never meant to be taken *literally.* Their interpretations were both scholarly and refreshing—not to mention *deeply reverent* toward God.

As time passed, I began to question the very *God* I was being taught about from fundamentalist and evangelical pulpits and lecterns; he seemed like such a tyrannical jerk. I began to believe that the very approach used by my evangelical and fundamentalist pastors/professors to interpret God's book was suspect. Their method was leading them to see a malevolent caricature of God—a deity who expresses conditional love, and motivates his worshippers through *fear.* These are universal hallmarks of abuse. I knew a different God from the angry and intractable version of God they constantly spoke of; I worshipped a God of second, third, and seventy-seventh chances.[11] I trusted a God who understood *existentially* what it is like to be human.[12] My God had a face—*Jesus.* I simply could not reconcile the wrathful ogre they spoke of with the Jesus I saw in the Gospels. Maybe you can relate?

---

10. The term used by people who take the Genesis creation account as literal fact, and who date the Earth to somewhere between six to ten thousand years old. Some who hold this position believe that God created the appearance of age to test our faith!

11. Matthew 18:22.

12. Hebrews 4:15.

I had many classmates who had exactly the same misgivings. We frequently spoke about our discomfort with the disconnect we perceived between what we were being taught and what we saw in Jesus in the pages of the New Testament. But most of them marched on. They *wanted* to fit in above all else. I don't fault them . . . too much. It is an uncomfortable struggle, one that's warned against from all positions of authority within fundamentalist and evangelical communities. Venturing into other theological understandings is presented as dangerous and potentially fatal to one's faith.

What made my path different was what I *did* with my doubts and questions. Instead of pretending they didn't exist, and tamping them down out of fear, I began exploring and researching them. I gave my doubts space to breathe. I wrote papers in my undergraduate classes exploring my distresses. I searched for other theories and understandings in different contemporary Christian communities. I dug into the writing of men and women from the distant past to find other explanations for those things that made me squirm. For example, as a sophomore I tackled women's ordination. Of course, in the mid 1980s all fundamentalists and most evangelicals rejected this idea out of hand. Most still do. But I wanted to know what the Bible and early church actually had to say; I wanted to know why some denominations had begun ordaining women. I had been told, "The Bible is clear . . . " and any church that was ordaining women plainly was doing it because they "reject the authority of the Scriptures."

It would have been convenient to discover that that was, in fact, the truth. But it was anything *but* the truth. Once I began talking with "them" face to face, I found these supposed "Bible-haters" actually *used* the Scriptures. They also pointed to mosaics and other historical evidence[13] to suggest the early church had in many places ordained women into the holy ministry![14] They suggested that female ordination was reasonably common for the first four centuries of Christianity. It seemed to have disappeared about the same time the church was becoming the official religion of the Roman Empire, a time when a lot of things were changing—mostly for the *worse!* They suggested that they were being *more* true to the Bible than those who didn't ordain women. That position squares with the actions

13. They used the science of archeology to flesh out their understanding of Scripture and provide context to aid our understanding of what was happening "on the ground" in the first couple of centuries of church history.

14. A fact that Pope Francis recently publically affirmed, even as he challenged the Roman Church to revisit the theology of the diaconate.

and attitudes of Jesus throughout the pages of the Gospels. After all, the person presented as first *proclaiming* Jesus as risen isn't a man, but Mary Magdalene.[15]

I learned this because I did something few of my colleagues dared to do: I went and listened to "them." I did this for a dozen or more issues that I wanted to explore with input from conservatives and liberals alike. I called and made appointments to interview several pastors from various traditions. I told them what issue I was exploring. I asked if I could sit down with them and discuss their personal (and their denomination's official) positions on the topic. I asked what other resources they could point me to. I asked each of them the same initial questions, took notes and posed follow up questions that were unique to each. Then I set to work comparing and contrasting the seven to ten points of view I gathered for every question I researched in this way. What I discovered was amazing: these "liberals" didn't hate God or the Bible nearly as much as I had been led to believe. In fact, most of them were pretty passionate about both! They just read and interpreted it all a bit differently from the ways I had been taught.

I was blessed to have professors who, though very "conservative" in their personal beliefs, were "liberal" enough to welcome this kind of approach. These professors were true scholars, and they helped me to become a good student. They were not always in agreement with my conclusions— generally they *weren't*—but none of them ever punished me academically for my conclusions, as long as my process was sound. I greatly appreciate that fact!

Curriculum Vitae

I've stated that I was trained as a fundamentalist and an evangelical. Now to firmly establish that fact:

In 1985 I graduated from Heritage Hall Christian School in Muncie, Indiana. This is a well-regarded day school in fundamentalist circles. Following high school, I attended Bob Jones University for a year. Yes, I went there! Most people don't know *that* about me. And it was there (in my mind, anyway) that the great *unwinding* began, and I began moving *left* on the theological scale.[16] It could have been any one of a thousand things that caused me to begin moving in a progressive direction, but it happened

15. John 20:17–18.

16. It would hardly be possible to move right from there!

to be the whole "no interracial dating" thing, in my case. I got caught up in it. One day I had a lunch in the BJU dining hall "with" a young Asian woman. I sat across the table from her and her sister with another White male student. And I got "turned in." I was summoned to the office of Tony Miller, dean of men. I was told to report the other students for similar punishment—something I couldn't do for the girls, because I didn't even know their names. I wasn't interested in them romantically. I was simply talking with them as human beings. And I refused to name my friend, the other guy. Nothing about the whole thing had been a date in my mind.

But that fact meant nothing to either Dr. Miller or me by the point I was sitting in his office. Dr. Miller told me that what I had done was most certainly a "sin." I had offended God by talking with one of the girls in particular (presumably because he was making this into some sort of forbidden romantic liaison). When I asked for a biblical reference establishing this as a sin, he cited 2 Corinthians 6:14: "Be ye not unequally yoked together . . . what communion hath light with darkness?" (KJV). Of course, when he *quoted* this passage to me the ellipsis was not so obvious. But I was familiar with the passage (an ironic "thank you" to HHCS!). The full passage reads: "Be ye not unequally yoked together with unbelievers: for what fellowship hath righteousness with unrighteousness? and what communion hath light with darkness?" I suggested the passage has an obvious *spiritual* context. Its scope is limited to partnerships (romantic and financial) between Christians and those who are most decidedly not. It has nothing to do with skin color.

I believe he was caught off guard by my retort. He agreed that "some" would argue that, but BJU took the passage more literally, *like God intended*. I also pointed out that both Moses and Solomon had married "Black" women according to the KJV. He was not amused. The rest of the scene unfolded as you might expect: I was officially blacklisted for disrespect. My (already) limited freedoms were seriously curtailed. And my name was included on an actual *list* posted in every dorm, labeling me as a discipline problem. It was a way to publically shame wayward students and "warn" all upright students to steer clear of me and my fellow ne'er-do-wells. But for me the cork was out of the bottle. My casual curiosity was now injected with the steroids of blatant hypocrisy.[17] I can literally remember thinking:

17. I wrote Dr. Miller a letter years later, after I saw him on national news denying BJU's dating policy was ever couched as "scriptural." They had recently relaxed it, in the wake of a George W. Bush campaign visit, which caused problems for him. They were dishonestly claiming it been presented solely as a "cultural practice," informed by their

"If they are willing to lie about the biblical rationale for this . . . what else are they lying to me about?"

I'm sure I became a positive menace as I began questioning many things that were prohibited, things that had sat uneasily with me for years: rock music, movies, playing cards, tobacco, alcohol, cursing, the democratic party . . . well, you get the point. I was on a quest. And what I learned in those first few months only inspired me to keep digging. Both what I had been told the Bible was "clear about," and what many of my teachers and pastors had claimed "science" says, were all seriously skewed. It didn't take much work in BJU's own library to determine that.

I completed my year at BJU and transferred to Cedarville College[18] (now University), in Ohio. This is where I found a more fertile ground for inquiry. I had examined many of the more superficial practices while at Bob Jones. At Cedarville I began to inquire into the very tenets of my faith. I examined the doctrines of election, free will, the atonement, communion, baptism and several others. This stuff is boring to most people, and I get that. But I loved it! I also began learning what *any* liberal arts student learns: how to read classical literature, a good bit about the history of world civilizations, some trig and calculus (and I've still never used either). I learned to tell the difference between Mozart, Beethoven and Dvorak; a bit about sociology, philosophy and the natural sciences. I read some Marx, and it wasn't what many think. I read Darwin's *Origin of Species* and I know it's not inconsistent with faith in God. I studied a bit of micro- and macroeconomics and some poly-sci. But mostly I learned that *nothing* is quite as simple as it seems at first glance. I learned to *think critically*. I learned that there's a lot that I don't know. And the more I learned, the more this became apparent. I learned that there are a lot of other ways to look at the world—and most of them are *no more right or wrong* than the way I had been taught to look at it. And that *is* the point of a liberal arts education!

I graduated in 1989, and went on to earn an MA in literature from Wright State University. Sensing God calling me to serve as a leader in his church, I continued on to Concordia Theological Seminary[19] to be more

South Carolina context. I reminded him of our afternoon together and the harsh punishment he had doled out to me. I never heard back from him.

18. A college aligned (at the time) with the very conservative General Association of Regular Baptist Churches (GARBC), and solidly on the right wing of the evangelical tradition.

19. One of two American seminaries of the Lutheran Church–Missouri Synod (LCMS), the only Lutheran body to generally be grouped with evangelicalism.

deeply trained in: Greek and Hebrew (the languages the books of the Bible were mostly written in); the struggles of the ancient church fathers, the Reformers and many other theologians between them and us about issues of faith, authority and our relationship with God; the evolution of church doctrine (and the shady way a lot of it happened![20]); congregational leadership and conflict resolution;[21] and a host of other things related to following Jesus and leading a local congregation.

I studied all this for an additional four years emerging with an MDiv, the standard academic degree for ministers. It has long been a tradition in most branches of the church to take very seriously the importance of pastors being educated as theological and ministry *professionals*. Accordingly, most established denominations require their pastors to hold both a BA or BS and an MDiv. Sensing the need for still further study in these dynamic times, I went on for another four years, earning the highest professional degree in church work, a DMin, from Trinity Episcopal School for Ministry[22] in Ambridge, Pennsylvania.

This *doesn't* mean that I "know it all." In fact, quite the *opposite*! I am genuinely humbled by how little I actually "know" for certain. And the more I've learned, the less rigid most of my "certainties" have become. Something that has grown *more certain*, however, is God's love for me. But that too has come at a "cost." As I have become increasingly confident of this love, it has become less *exclusive*. The more I realize how much God loves me, the more I realize he loves absolutely everyone else on Earth with the same vitality. This has been a vital driver for my journey from fundamentalism (which is pretty tribal, by definition), into moderate progressivism (which is always focused on humanity as one family). Along the way, I read books by men and women that drove me to anger and bewilderment, because their faith is so different from mine. Yet I have learned from them, and I have seen them produce fruit for the kingdom of God. I've marveled to observe God bless

20. For example, St. Nicholas (aka Santa Claus), bishop of Myra, attended the First Council of Nicaea in 325 CE. He is famously purported to have punched another bishop, Arius, in the nose. In response a third bishop, Eusebius, is said to have urinated on Nicholas. However, after a short time in the dungeon, Nicholas "miraculously" escaped and returned to the deliberations. He claimed that the Holy Mother freed him and favored his doctrinal position over Arius's. He carried the day, and the Nicene Creed reflects his position. You can't make this stuff up . . . *anymore*!

21. A course Nicholas, Arius, and Eusebius could have benefitted from.

22. This seminary has since suspended general use of "Episcopal" from its name to clarify its independence from the Episcopal Church in the USA.

their efforts. I have been reminded repeatedly of Mark 9:38–41: "John said to him, 'Teacher, we saw someone casting out demons in your name, and we tried to stop him, because he was not following us.' But Jesus said, 'Do not stop him; for no one who does a deed of power in my name will be able soon afterward to speak evil of me. Whoever is not against us is for us. For truly I tell you, whoever gives you a cup of water to drink because you bear the name of Christ will by no means lose the reward.'" And I have become more *humbled*.

I have listened to sermons and lectures by Christians from places far removed from my context (or just next door) that have opened a world of possibilities I could never have imagined on my own. I have been blessed and expanded by the thoughts and experiences of preachers who are different from me. But I see Christ in them and their views, even when they have conflicted with my own. And I have widened my views to make room for theirs. Almost all of my convictions have been challenged and changed because I have wrestled with thoughts and opinions that differ from what I once believed was settled fact. I have learned to *judge* a lot less, and to *consider* a lot more. I have been forced to modify many of my unquestioned presuppositions—most of which I didn't even realize I held, until someone came along and unraveled them. All of this has driven me back to the Scriptures myriad times.

I've looked at all the familiar texts again, with new eyes . . . and usually in the original languages. I've considered how English translations have rendered passages over the ages. I've sought to figure out *why*. I've also learned to apply texts I'd omitted (either from ignorance or, more often, *convenience*) from my thought matrix. And I've learned that passages that, on the surface, may not seem to apply to a given issue sometimes have a great deal to offer. I've learned that, if you pay close attention, Jesus *rarely* actually answers questions—at least not the ones people ask him. And I've noticed he's more likely to "answer" by asking yet another question. And it has occurred to me that this fact is actually quite important. Our Lord seems far less concerned with *factoid* ripostes and much more focused on very nuanced responses rooted in compassion and respect for others—even our enemies.

Over the course of my journey I've moved from the "religious right" to the center and well into the "religious left." However, far from destroying my faith, the left has nurtured my trust in a *good* God. It has freed me from the compulsion to believe there's only one valid theological point of view.

The left has emancipated me from fastidiously *avoiding* "wrong" actions, or even their "appearance." It has released me to enjoy a *relationship* with God that's built on his unconditional love of me and everyone else.

Embracing this love is liberating, and it's allowed me to divert my focus from myself and fix it on others. Instead of needing to impress God, or meticulously fend off his wrath with scrupulous observance of manufactured codes of conduct, I am free to *be* a son of God. And because God has made me his child, that has freed me to express care and concern for others in ways I never experienced before. Luther puts it this way: "God does not need your good works, but your neighbor does."[23] I believe that I best serve *God* when I am working to bless *the people around me.* Instead of caring because I'm commanded to, I am compelled (inwardly) to care because I see others as *people whom God loves* just as much as he loves me.

My goal in writing is to present a picture of Christian discipleship that is alive and dynamic. One that's driven by an abiding trust in God who has adopted us, instead of by rules or platitudes. I believe God wants each of us to actually *be like Jesus,* starting with our hearts and working outward. I hope to reclaim words like "moderate" and "liberal" as *positive* words for Christians to embody. The bulk of this book will be divided into conversations about two core differences between evangelicalism and fundamentalism, on one hand, and what I believe is a truer form of Christianity, on the other.

The religious right and left in this country comprehend *Scripture* differently, and they differ in their understanding of Christ's *kingdom.* These two differences lead to many—perhaps most—of the other more obvious dissimilarities between them. On the one hand, the different ways each reverences Scripture explains why a *literal* seven-day creation is vital to one, while evolution can be embraced as God's process in the other. It explains the fervor of the anti-abortion movement in the former, and the more tempered approach in the latter. It's why fundamentalists and evangelicals are so opposed to homosexuality and why many mainline clergy are free to bless these unions in their churches.

The second distinction, concerning the ways the two groups conceive of Christ's kingdom, also yields dramatically different results. It's why evangelicals and fundamentalists are so much more . . . well, "evangelistic" in their worship services and in their communities. It's why they are so driven to "get people saved," while mainline Christians tend to view salvation

23. Wingren, *Luther on Vocation,* 10.

more as a relationship, and therefore a dynamic process whose eternal consequences are much less stark. It's why evangelicals and fundamentalists focus so much on the "rapture," and a *future* thousand-year reign of Christ, while most moderates consider the kingdom to be a *present* reality. It's why evangelicals and fundamentalists are so keen on the Ten Commandments, while the Beatitudes are more popular among progressive believers.

As you read the thoughts expressed on the following pages I hope you'll consider whether they reflect Jesus' teaching. Ask yourself if the sermons and positions of your congregation do the same. As Christians, we're called to follow the Messiah in thought, word and deed. Obviously, none of us will ever do that perfectly, but we are called to try nonetheless. That means we need to be evaluating ourselves in light of him. It also means we need to be actively striving to build his kingdom reality in our world.

1

"Fairy Tales" Aren't Just for Children

Fairy tales don't tell children that dragons exist.
Children already know that dragons exist.
Fairy tales tell children that dragons can be killed.

—*CRIMINAL MINDS*[1]

For too long we've read the scriptures with
nineteenth-century eyes and sixteenth-century questions.
It's time we get back to reading with
first-century eyes and twenty-first-century questions.

—N. T. WRIGHT[2]

WHAT'S THE BIBLE GOOD for? Does it speak *authoritatively* about: God? Humanity? Science? History? Theology? Politics? Self-improvement? Dieting? Psychology? Medicine? Dating? Finances? Morality? It's a complex question to most of us . . . but *not* to some. We probably all know someone who thinks, "The Bible says it, and that settles it!"

I recently read that on a bumper sticker, which is decidedly *not* the best source from which to draw your theology. You've probably encountered similar platitudes. The problem with oversimplifications like this is

1. *Criminal Minds*, "Seven Seconds."
2. Wright, *Justification*, 37.

the Bible is a highly *complex* book—*several* complex books gathered under one cover, actually. And while all these books are important, they are not all the same. As shocking as this is for some people to discover, the various books contained in the Bible don't even always agree with each other. For instance, Moses gives us a law of *proportional response*: "Anyone who maims another shall suffer the same injury in return: fracture for fracture, eye for eye, tooth for tooth; the injury inflicted is the injury to be suffered."[3] But Jesus emphatically *rejects* this ethic. One of the things that made the priests and rabbis dislike (hate) Jesus was the fact that he felt free to *correct* Moses and the Torah. Jesus proposed a radically *different morality* from the one Israel had embraced for well over a millennium. He cites this passage in his Sermon on the Mount and significantly alters it. Jesus says: "You have heard that it was said, 'An eye for an eye and a tooth for a tooth.' But I say to you, do not resist an evildoer. But if anyone strikes you on the right cheek, turn the other also; and if anyone wants to sue you and take your coat, give your cloak as well; and if anyone forces you to go one mile, go also the second mile. Give to everyone who begs from you, and do not refuse anyone who wants to borrow from you."[4] That's fundamentally different from Moses' ethic. It evidences an evolution in our understanding of God, and what is expected of us as his people.

Other "contradictions" found in the pages of the Bible are the fruit of an overly literalistic reading of the text—how many men (or angels) appeared to the women at the tomb on the morning of the resurrection?: one man in Mark 16:5; one angel in Matthew 28:2; two men in Luke 24:4; two angels in John 20:12. The imperative question is, *"Does it really matter?"* And more importantly, *why* are these figures inserted into the story at all— what *function* do they serve? The point of all four accounts is clearly not the number (or physiology) of whomever these figures are. What's important is that they draw attention to the *empty tomb*. The theme of the story is the resurrection of Jesus. These men or angels are literary *sentinels* to that. *That's what changes everything.* At least that's the point for people who share my more "liberal" view of Scripture. But if you have bought into the propaganda about biblical "inerrancy" and "infallibility,"[5] these passages present something of a conundrum!

3. Leviticus 24:19–20.

4. Matthew 5:38–42.

5. Buzz words that many Christians embrace, not realizing that the Bible never asserts either of these notions.

This *crucial moment* in religious history is more than a bit *convoluted*, at least in terms of the *details* the surrounding the story. Throughout the resurrection accounts in the Gospels we see *differences*—some quite significant. The order of events, various specifics, who is (or isn't) present at various junctures, what they do (or don't do), and where they're told to meet up with the risen Lord all differ—to the point of being contradictory in places.[6]

Can they be made to fit together? Of course, with a little "massaging" and creativity. One might think that the four Gospel writers would have compared notes and gotten the details a bit more in sync with each other—especially since nearly everyone agrees that the writers of Matthew[7] and Luke both borrowed heavily from the Gospel of Mark. Irregularities become even more critical if one believes the Bible offers an "inerrant" and "infallible" account of the most significant event recorded in its pages. But instead the writers of both Matthew and Luke *tweak* Mark's account and put their spin on it for their own purposes. And John tells the story from an entirely different point of view. And the results are different.

A man named Tatian tried to smooth out the wrinkles around 170 CE. He consolidated the events of the Gospels into a *single* work *without variation*—a kind of composite Gospel. He called his work the *Diatessaron*. All the other church fathers *rejected* his harmonized and sanitized Gospel account. They believed the Gospels were doing something other than offering a newspaper account of the history of Jesus. They believed the differences and contradictions between accounts weren't a hindrance to their true purpose. Let's take a moment and simply read the resurrection accounts from each source, in the order they were most likely written:

Mark 16:1–8

When the sabbath was over, Mary Magdalene, and Mary the mother of James, and Salome bought spices, so that they might go and anoint him. And very early on the first day of the week, when the sun had risen, they went to the tomb. They had been saying to one another, "Who will roll away

6. Mark 16:8 says the women "said nothing to anyone." Luke 24:9 insists they went to the eleven (and "the rest") and "told" them about their encounter with the two men "in dazzling white." John suggests that only Mary Magdalene went. Mark and Matthew move the eleven to Galilee to meet the risen Jesus, while Luke leaves them in Jerusalem.

7. The Bible never actually asserts that the Gospel of Matthew was written by a man called Matthew, let alone *the* Matthew of the circle of apostles—that name was applied to the Gospel later on. It's simply a pious tradition.

the stone for us from the entrance to the tomb?" When they looked up, they saw that the stone, which was very large, had already been rolled back. As they entered the tomb, they saw a young man, dressed in a white robe, sitting on the right side; and they were alarmed. But he said to them, "Do not be alarmed; you are looking for Jesus of Nazareth, who was crucified. He has been raised; he is not here. Look, there is the place they laid him. But go, tell his disciples and Peter that he is going ahead of you to Galilee; there you will see him, just as he told you." So they went out and fled from the tomb, for terror and amazement had seized them; and they said nothing to anyone, for they were afraid.

Matthew 28:1–10

After the sabbath, as the first day of the week was dawning, Mary Magdalene and the other Mary went to see the tomb. And suddenly there was a great earthquake; for an angel of the Lord, descending from heaven, came and rolled back the stone and sat on it. His appearance was like lightning, and his clothing white as snow. For fear of him the guards shook and became like dead men. But the angel said to the women, "Do not be afraid; I know that you are looking for Jesus who was crucified. He is not here; for he has been raised, as he said. Come, see the place where he lay. Then go quickly and tell his disciples, 'He has been raised from the dead, and indeed he is going ahead of you to Galilee; there you will see him.' This is my message for you." So they left the tomb quickly with fear and great joy, and ran to tell his disciples. Suddenly Jesus met them and said, "Greetings!" And they came to him, took hold of his feet, and worshiped him. Then Jesus said to them, "Do not be afraid; go and tell my brothers to go to Galilee; there they will see me."

Luke 24:1–12

But on the first day of the week, at early dawn, they came to the tomb, taking the spices that they had prepared. They found the stone rolled away from the tomb, but when they went in, they did not find the body. While they were perplexed about this, suddenly two men in dazzling clothes stood beside them. The women were terrified and bowed their faces to the ground, but the men said to them, "Why do you look for the living among the dead? He is not here, but has risen. Remember how he told you, while he was still in Galilee, that the Son of Man must be handed over to sinners, and be crucified, and on the third day rise again." Then they remembered his words, and returning from the tomb, they told all this to the eleven and to all the rest. Now it was Mary Magdalene, Joanna, Mary the mother of James, and the other women with them who told this to the apostles. But these words seemed to them an idle tale, and they did not believe them. But Peter got up and ran to the tomb; stooping and looking in, he saw the linen cloths by themselves; then he went home, amazed at what had happened.

John 20:1–16

Early on the first day of the week, while it was still dark, Mary Magdalene came to the tomb and saw that the stone had been removed from the tomb. So she ran and went to Simon Peter and the other disciple, the one whom Jesus loved, and said to them, "They have taken the Lord out of the tomb, and we do not know where they have laid him." Then Peter and the other disciple set out and went toward the tomb. The two were running together, but the other disciple outran Peter and reached the tomb first. He bent down to look in and saw the linen wrappings lying there, but he did not go in. Then Simon Peter came, following him, and went into the tomb. He saw the linen wrappings lying there, and the cloth that had been on Jesus' head, not lying with the linen wrappings but rolled up in a place by itself. Then the other disciple, who reached the tomb first, also went in, and he saw and believed; for as yet they did not understand the Scripture, that he must rise from the dead. Then the disciples returned to their homes. But Mary stood weeping outside the tomb. As she wept, she bent over to look into the tomb; and she saw two angels in white, sitting where the body of Jesus had been lying, one at the head and the other at the feet. They said to her, "Woman, why are you weeping?" She said to them, "They have taken away my Lord, and I do not know where they have laid him." When she had said this, she turned around and saw Jesus standing there, but she did not know that it was Jesus. Jesus said to her, "Woman, why are you weeping? Whom are you looking for?" Supposing him to be the gardener, she said to him, "Sir, if you have carried him away, tell me where you have laid him, and I will take him away." Jesus said to her, "Mary!" She turned and said to him in Hebrew, "Rabbouni!" (which means Teacher).

The accounts are all *similar* . . . yet they're *different* too. How many women were there? Who were they? Did they or didn't they tell anyone about what they had seen and heard? And was it Peter, or Peter and "the disciple who Jesus loved"[8] whom they spoke with (or didn't!)? Did Jesus speak with all the women, or Mary Magdalene alone? And what about the soldiers? There are several details that are quite different, and a few that are just plain contradictory.

First-century people didn't operate under the same rules that we use as they told (and retold) stories of this sort. We tend to expect every fact and detail to be *literally* true as it's presented. We want a story like the resurrection to be relayed as though it were a transcript of a trial—just the facts and only the facts, as they actually happened in space and time. But first-century people *didn't* always do things that way. They told stories to convey what (literally) happened, but *also* (and *more* importantly) to express the theological, emotional, and political *ramifications* of those events. They *interpreted* the impact of events, as they understood them as a part of the story.

In the mid-twentieth century, Rudolf Bultmann recognized this disconnect; he began "demythologizing" the Bible in an attempt to bridge the gap created by our modern expectations. He noted that the Bible, with its laxness in regard to exact places, times, and people, was addressing questions in a style in which we are no longer fluent. He believed we needed to focus our attention on the "thatness" of Jesus and hold more loosely to the "whatness," because the biblical writers exercised so little precision in those sorts of details. He was on to something very important, something central to the worldview of first-century people. The Bible is an ancient document, written to *ancient* people, following the rules and expectations of *its age*. To expect it to behave like a twenty-first-century historical document is foolish! We have a word for this kind of thing: *anachronism*. That means importing our understanding of things back in time onto things that came long before us. People do it all the time; especially with the Bible.

The Bible is chock full of metaphors cover to cover. That doesn't mean the things it talks about didn't happen, though some of them certainly didn't. The Bible's aim is to impart *truth*, not necessarily facts. Literarily the job of metaphors is to teach truth, but not through literalism.

You've probably heard the quote, "Sometimes a cigar is just a cigar." At about the same time Bultmann was stressing the importance of a more

---

8. A figure who first shows up at the Last Supper in John's Gospel. He's sometimes thought to be the Apostle John, though this seems unlikely. Other surmises include Jesus' brother James, Mary Magdalene, or Lazarus after he was raised by Jesus. A few scholars even suggest this figure is a metaphor for the church. I favor the Lazarus theory.

symbolic interpretation of Scripture, Sigmund Freud was founding a branch of psychology called psychoanalysis. He believed that we all have deeply suppressed feelings and pains. We're often not even fully aware of them. According to Freud these buried emotions often manifest themselves to our conscious selves in symbolic ways. Freud taught his students to probe these manifestations to uncover the deeper truth their patients' subconscious minds were trying to reveal. His students began *overreading* symbolic expressions in everything the people around them did. They even suggested Freud's love of cigar smoking had a deeper meaning that he needed to explore . . . hence the quote.

Psychoanalysis and demythologizing came on the scene in the midst of the Enlightenment Era, a time when the place of *symbol* and *metaphor* had essentially been stripped out of life. "Realism" was the order of the day; humanity was being urged to embrace life like Spock in *Star Trek*, or Joe Friday of *Dragnet*, men who viewed life in stark relief, grasping only "the facts." This notion was rooted in another myth: objective truth. It's something that the physicist Werner Heisenberg later showed to be an utter impossibility.

Remember when the French phrase "Je suis Charlie!" was everywhere? It means: "I am Charlie." Signs saying this appeared worldwide following a mass shooting at the headquarters of the newspaper *Charlie Hebdo* in Paris, on January 7, 2015. Obviously, none of the people holding those placards *were* Charlie Hebdo—there isn't any such person! But people can identify with the *ideals* such a paper holds within society. They opposed the violence of those who wished to silence free thought and expression by standing in solidarity with *Charlie Hebdo*. They did that by holding signs claiming to *be* "Charlie." That is easy enough to understand.

Now think of Adam and Eve. I suggest to you that they never existed as two literal individuals;[9] yet they live on in each of us. They *are* you and me, and everyone else who's ever lived. I suggest the Bible *never intended* them to be taken as actual individuals. That's something that happened *millennia* after the story was recorded. It happened when people began thinking more literally and less figuratively. It happened as people began divorcing themselves from mystery in favor of the pretense of "objectivity."

There are some real advantages to a hyper-realistic approach to things: science, medicine, geography, and engineering have all benefitted enormously from the Enlightenment's laser focus on details and precision. And

---

9. We will discuss this at much greater length in chapter 3.

humanity has benefitted. But there has been a trade-off. We've lost a lot of richness and beauty. We've forgotten how to read the Bible as if it were a living text in which God speaks (breathes) to us through symbols. We've turned it into a *textbook* from which to mine "facts," trivia, and find some morality.

And in case you think no one would actually suggest the Bible is a textbook on science or anything else, I'll cite a tweet from leading evangelical "scientist" Ken Ham:

> Ken Ham, @aigkenham
> The Bible is actually a textbook of historical science—and the only such textbook that is totally reliable and infallible.
> 5:35 p.m., January 3, 2017

You may have watched the debate between Ken Ham and Bill Nye "the Science Guy" on February 4, 2014. In that discussion Ham stated emphatically that there was absolutely no evidence that could convince him to change his mind about his beliefs regarding Genesis. He might as well have said, "Don't bother me with facts, my mind is made up."

The same time Bultmann was demythologizing the Bible, Freud was exploring the importance of symbols in our subconscious minds, and existentialism[10] was gaining ascendancy in many churches in Europe and America, the original "fundamentalists" were *pushing back*. In 1917 a book was published which set forth ninty essays that all "true Christians" should affirm. It was simply called *The Fundamentals*.[11] Among other things, the book soundly condemned "higher criticism," a methodology of biblical interpretation that employs modern techniques to approximate what words and passages may have crept into biblical texts long after the original books were written. It is the science that aids scholars and ministers in reading the Bible more like first-century people would have. *The Fundamentals* rejects all forms of "modernism" like this as departures from God's will. Proponents regard all tools of scholarship, science, psychology, and archeology (that don't support a *literal* recounting what the Bible reports) as sinful. The authors *especially* condemn the theory of evolution as faith destroying. *The*

10. Belief that individuals are free agents, determining their own course in life through choices and experiences.

11. Dixon and Torrey, *The Fundamentals*.

Fundamentals propose, instead, a total commitment to the Bible as "infallible." The original fundamentalists insisted the Bible could never change. In fact they insisted it *had* never changed. Further, they contend, the books of the Bible have been transmitted to us nearly totally without alteration. And any *proof* that demonstrates that Scripture has changed[12] is simply denied as a liberal stratagem to destroy the true faith.

It never seems to have occurred to devotees of this model that it's *their method* of interpretation which has changed, not the Bible.[13] Dominic Crossan has said: "My point . . . is not that those ancient people told literal stories and we are now smart enough to take them symbolically, but that they told them symbolically and we are now dumb enough to take them literally."[14] Evangelical and fundamentalist interpretation techniques are an example of anachronistic thinking. They use *modern expectations* to guide their understanding of an *ancient text*. The results are tragic!

Literalistic thinking (and preaching) has also led to books on how to eat according to God's will.[15] It's given us a couple of volumes on how to date (or "court") like God intends.[16] And it has yielded at least one book on how to be the kind of business manager that Jesus was,[17] as if *that* is the message of the Christ! This kind of preaching, and the thinking that lies behind it, seriously warps what the scriptural authors were actually trying to communicate to their audience. There are literally hundreds of passages in the Bible that tell us that God is long-suffering and merciful, and that "righteousness" is tied to generosity to the needy, particularly the widow and

12. And there is lots of it!

13 Coincidently the fundamentalist assertion of biblical infallibility occurred at about the same time Roman Catholics professed papal infallibility. The West was experiencing a crisis of authority, and these "infallibilities" salved that anxiety. Democratization that valued all people's thoughts was also emerging. *Both* doctrines of infallibility were dispatched to quash as much of that as possible too, preserving the authority and privilege of the clergy class.

14. Crossan, *Who Is Jesus?*, 79.

15. Burgher, *The Creator's Diet*; Halliday, *Hunger Within: A Biblical Approach to Weight Management*; Gregory and Bloomer, *The Daniel Cure: The Daniel Fast Way to Vibrant Health*; Kennedy, *The Heart Health Bible: The 5-Step Plan to Prevent and Reverse Heart Disease*; Rossner, *Eating the Bible*. These are just a few examples of books based on the idea that what people ate in the Bible is *prescriptive* in some fashion for us today. There are dozens of others!

16. Gundersen, *Courtship and Dating: So What's the Difference*; Harris, *I Kissed Dating Goodbye* and *Boy meets Girl: Say Hello to Courtship*.

17. Jones, *Jesus CEO*.

orphan. This is the recurring theme of Isaiah, Jeremiah, and all the Minor Prophets. It's an attitude commonly present in the Torah. And it's a constant refrain of Jesus himself. However, it is not a theme commonly preached in most evangelical or fundamentalist congregations. Their preachers are far more likely to preach *against* what they see as moral erosion in our nation—especially the rise in *acceptance* of: homosexuality,[18] the equality of females to males,[19] or the benefits of multiculturalism.[20] Each of these are examples of the (healthy) erosion of White patriarchy being mistaken for a rejection of God himself. They aren't the same thing![21]

In 1978, the heirs of the original (1917) fundamentalist movement gathered in Chicago and released the "Chicago Statement on Biblical Inerrancy." This term—*inerrancy*—has become central to the debate on what the Bible is today. It has nearly become a battle cry. The Chicago document states that the Bible "is infallible . . . it is true and reliable in all matters it addresses."[22] Essentially the nearly three hundred signers of this document committed to continuing to read a first-century document *anachronistically*, with twentieth-century eyes. Their contemporary followers continue to condemn anyone who differs from them, and their *literalistic* approach to the Bible—an approach that has the inconvenient consequence of including nearly all preachers for the first 1400 years of church history!

However, the biggest flaw in their position, which is overlooked by both the original "fundamentalists" and the later Chicago group, is that the Bible itself never claims anything like "inerrancy" as they define it. Nor does it claim to be "infallible." The verses that best describe the Bible's *self-understanding* are: "[Y]ou have known the Holy Scriptures, which are able

18. Something the Bible only tangentially mentions six times, and never in reference to consensual relations between committed peers.

19. Under the guise of "complementarianism," many evangelicals and fundamentalists stress an essential difference between the sexes, which they codify as a "biblical mandate" inherent in creation and reflected in Western gender roles, including the idea that the male is the "head" of the female.

20. Which several evangelicals and fundamentalists equate to a "war cry" against godly, White, Western patriarchy.

21. In many circles, if a person disagrees with their evangelical or fundamentalist pastor's "official" take on these things (and countless others), then he or she is generally (*ipso facto*) regarded as a Bible denier and a God hater. It's an effective way to control discussion and assure one's preferred outcome is the *only* possible "biblical" outcome. It also amounts to bullying. And it's wrong.

22. International Council on Biblical Inerrancy, "Chicago Statement on Biblical Inerrancy," 4.

to make you wise for salvation through faith in Christ Jesus. All Scripture is God-breathed and is useful for teaching, rebuking, correcting and training in righteousness, so that the servant of God may be thoroughly equipped for every good work."[23] And: "So we have the prophetic message more fully confirmed. You will do well to be attentive to this as to a lamp shining in a dark place, until the day dawns and the morning star rises in your hearts. First of all you must understand this, that no prophecy of Scripture is a matter of one's own interpretation, because no prophecy ever had its origin in the human will, but prophets, though human, spoke from God as they were carried along by the Holy Spirit."[24] That's it. That's what the Bible claims for *itself*. Moved

You'll note that the two key words the Religious Right incessantly claim for the Bible (inerrant & infallible) are not present. In their place the only biblical passages that address the authority of the written Scripture say that it is "God-breathed" and that the prophetic writers were "carried along" in the process of writing. Another word for this is "inspired," a word linked to "breath." The Bible simply claims to be "God-breathed."

When one views the Bible as "inspired," and that prophets were "moved" by the Holy Spirit, the resulting text can be seen as containing some limitations. A person embracing *this* standard will end up viewing the Bible differently from someone who believes that the text is *literally true* on every level, and *wholly without error* on every matter it addresses. The latter person makes the Bible a virtual god of its own, while the former will see it as a vehicle, a place where God walks among people, revealing himself[25] as they (we) are able to see him.

I realize that this concept can be unsettling to those who have been accustomed to thinking that the Bible is more than it actually claims to be. I began this chapter with a quote: "Fairy tales don't tell children that dragons exist. Children already know that dragons exist. Fairy tales tell children that dragons can be killed."[26] I chose it for a couple of reasons. First, it suggests a better approach for interpreting Scripture. Ancient holy texts do not approach life the way we do in the twenty-first century. That's not a value

23. 1 Timothy 3:15b–17.

24. 2 Peter 1:19–21.

25. Gender is one of those limitations! Certainly God is no more male than female, and encompasses both. Yet, sometimes we are limited by our language to pick a pronoun to reflect that reality!

26. *Criminal Minds*, "Seven Seconds."

judgment. They are no more right or wrong than us; they just do things differently. I believe this distinction is lost on many (most) fundamentalists and evangelicals today. Most are guilty of coming to the text anachronistically. In the case of Genesis, they read it as "science." They contend that Moses wrote about 2,500 years ago by virtual dictation. They believe, for instance, that the book of Genesis offers us God's literal and historical account of creation. This is why fanatics like Ken Ham will spend $100 million reconstructing an ark—a boat which uses modern steel and wood laminates precisely because such a structure *literally* can't support its own enormous weight with Bible-time building supplies! And that's true when it's resting on solid ground. When placed on water, such a structure would immediately break apart. And on some level they know that! But they demand acquiescence anyway.[27] But enthusiasts of a literal ark preach their anti-intellectual message and call into question the *faith* of anyone who points out the obvious scientific problems with their biblical literalism. But it's all just silly! It's grounded on a literalism that's wholly manufactured. They *misunderstand* what this passage was inspired to teach us.

There is another way—a way a person can take the Scriptures seriously while still embracing scientific facts. There's a way of interpreting the Bible that doesn't require a *deus ex machina*[28] to ride in and save the day by superseding the laws of nature, a way that we can synthesize the ancient text of the Bible with modern science. The answer lies in learning to read the Bible the way people would have approached it two thousand years ago[29] (and before that). Two millennia ago people viewed Scripture as more symbolic than literal. We need to recognize that the Bible teaches us *truth* through parable, symbol, and story. The point is rarely the story itself, but the *truth* behind it. This is how we approach all other literature, but somehow the fact that Scripture is literature has gotten lost for some.

27. Less well known (in America) is the fact that Ken Ham's ark is at least the second modern attempt to reconstruct Noah's famous boat. Dutchman Johan Huibers did essentially the same thing in his homeland in 2012. His full-size replica rests in the water on twenty-five steel barges, welded together to form a single steel hull. He used steel barges as the base for the same reason Ham built his boat out of steel and plywood: that's the only way such a structure can possibly hold together on water.

28. A Latin phrase coined by Aristotle meaning "god from the machine." It was a common plot device in ancient plays whereby an unsolvable problem is rectified by divine intervention. It was thought to show a lack of creativity on the part of the author by most critics. It's no different in biblical exegesis!

29. The vast majority of early church fathers did not interpret the creation account literally.

The second reason I selected the quote is because it is a perfect example of textual change. The *original* G. K. Chesterton quote was this: "Fairy tales do not give the child his first idea of bogey. What fairy tales give the child is his first clear idea of the possible defeat of bogey."[30] Chesterton is a brilliant writer but this quote isn't nearly as memorable as the one at the head of this chapter. And it uses the strange word "bogey." Who even knows what that is! It sounds more like an enemy plane than a dragon. But there's more to the story. The line above didn't come to us directly from Chesterton's quip. A man named Neil Gaiman wrote a book called *Coraline* in 2002. He included Chesterton's witty quote, without looking it up.[31] He pinned what he *remembered* of it: "Fairy tales are more than true—not because they tell us dragons exist, but because they tell us dragons can be beaten."[32] At the hands of the writers of *Criminal Minds* it becomes: "Fairy tales don't tell children that dragons exist. Children already know that dragons exist. Fairy tales tell children that dragons can be killed." And so you have it: a famous quote, relaying a truth originally pinned by G. K. Chesterton, altered (and improved) by Neil Gaiman, which is further polished by the writers of *Criminal Minds*. And that's a crash course in textual criticism! This quote is an actual example of how at least three writers have labored to convey the same truth. Starting with one set of words, others altered them to produce a text that resonates to our day. Two hundred years from now someone else may come along and make it better for that time. Denying that the scriptural text has changed over time—at some points dramatically—is an example of reveling in ignorance and calling it virtue.

Scripture is God breathed and is useful for forming our teaching and beliefs (doctrine) as Christian people. It is beneficial as a source in instructing us in how to embody our trust in God through Christ in this fallen world. It's valuable in communicating God's love to us (and others). The Bible, however, is not a history book, as we understand history texts. The Bible isn't a guide on how to eat right, manage your money, or find self-fulfillment! It isn't a good science text or medical reference—not if you want to avoid germs and infections. God never intended us to look to this book for those sorts of things. In 2 Peter the Bible claims simply to be a light shining in the dark. It points toward Christ; but it is not the same thing

30. Chesterton, *Tremendous Trifles*, 130.

31. Wood, "Neil Gaiman on the Meaning of Fairy Tales."

32. Gaiman, *Coraline*, epigraph.

as Jesus. According to John 1, Jesus is "the Word" . . . the Bible isn't, even though we sometimes call it that.

For this reason it doesn't matter if the Bible gets a date wrong or refers to a place which is not quite where the Bible says it was. It doesn't really matter that the Scripture says the mustard seed is the smallest of all seeds when that is demonstrably not true, because that's not what its *purpose* is. We should look to the Bible for *spiritual* truth. Not for dating advice, or to learn how to "eat like Jesus," or for financial guidance. Pastors should not preach sermon series on "seven simple Bible steps to improve your sex life." And I wish I were kidding, but pastors around the country are doing stuff like this regularly today. The Bible doesn't speak *authoritatively* about these matters. We do well to remember that. We do better to see the Bible as the breath of God: a place God joins us, walking among us, revealing himself as we are able to see him.

How many muses are there?
What are their names?

handwritten marginalia: Who wrote Hebrews? Apollos? Priscilla? Aquila? Barnabas?

2

A Uniquely American Error

A fearful Christian is a person who has not understood the message of Jesus.
—POPE FRANCIS[1]

There is a cult of ignorance in the United States, and there always has been. The strain of anti-intellectualism has been a constant thread winding its way through our political and cultural life, nurtured by the false notion that democracy means that "my ignorance is just as good as your knowledge."
—ISAAC ASIMOV[2]

HAVE YOU NOTICED THAT many, perhaps *most*, fundamentalists and evangelicals believe all of the events recorded in the Old Testament are *actual* and *literal* history? They believe when the children of Israel obey all of God's rules he responds by blessing them with good harvests, peace, and prosperity. And whenever a sufficiently high number disobey the 613 rules of the Old Testament, God punishes them with drought, pestilence, or war. Yet most of these brothers and sisters fail to realize that such a scenario is the very *definition* of "conditional love."

1. As quoted by Schneible, "Pope Francis: Fear and Joylessness."
2. Asimov, "Cult of Ignorance."

Their understanding of Scripture converts God into an *abusive* parent, who only expresses love when we march in lockstep with his demands. Put another way, they believe God's *holiness* supersedes his *love*.[3] They think keeping his "rules" is the key to getting him to show affection and bless us with his goodwill. It's monstrous!

Unfortunately they aren't content to leave this conditional "love" deep in the past. Many continue to express it in the sermons they preach every week all across the country—everything from pronouncements of God's wrath on cities in the form of natural disasters for some perceived sin, to statements like this one I heard firsthand in the early 1980s: "God expects all Christians to tithe. And God always gets what he wants. So you might as well give him his 10 percent in the offering plate, or he'll find another way to take it. He'll break down your car, or make you sick. Listen to me now; he's going to get what's his, so you're better off just giving it to him right now, than risking how he comes after it."[4] I have no doubt that the pastor who said this really believed it. *His God* works this way. But nothing like this comes from Jesus, who "Is the reflection of God's glory and the exact imprint of God's very being,"[5] and "The image of the invisible God . . . [in whom] all the fullness of God was pleased to dwell."[6]

Holy books are sacred *guides* that speak from an ancient context but are still powerfully relevant to our day. But mining truth from them is a complicated process. The Bible is at times internally contradictory. At others it reflects the norms and values of primeval people—values that are often difficult to defend from our standpoint, like slavery or even genocide. Both are examples that the Bible embraces and even commands in some passages! Have you ever read one of those passages? Did you have difficulty reconciling it with Jesus?

But many people insist on reading the Bible literally, despite the cognitive dissonance this causes. Simplifying the Scriptures works! It *simplifies* "discipleship." It removes many of the *grey areas* of life, and makes being a "follower of Jesus" as simple as getting the right list of rules and then

---

3. We'll return to this in chapter 8.

4. I can't say this is a perfectly accurate quote, but it is exactly the spirit of what was said—and the bits about the broken-down car and getting sick are the exact examples the preacher used.

5. Hebrews 1:3.

6. Colossians 1:15, 19.

following them.[7] That's so much easier than the more ambiguous lifestyle that Jesus *actually* calls us to, with its internal contradictions and tensions. And millions of Americans gobble it up . . . right up until it does one of two things to them: it burns them up, because they just *can't* seem to get it "right," so they develop *contempt* for this onerous God; or it burns them up because they *can*, and they slowly grow *contempt* for their fellow travelers who can't get their act together. Neither of these scenarios resembles Jesus. And yet both are common results in American fundamentalism and evangelicalism. It has become the stuff of American church folklore. That's why it's so difficult to resist!

Somehow the church in America got hijacked. At least her *expectations* have been. We live in a *Funda-gelical Industrial Complex*—and even without looking it up, I'm pretty certain I just coined that term. But there's more truth to it than you may know! *Unlike* most "industrial complexes," the power of this one does *not* just reside with a few religious leaders who pull strings and exert outsized influence at the expense of both lay people and less prominent clergy; the power of this one resides deep in our American psyche too. One might say it was in our DNA from our founding.

Theological developments occurred at our nation's founding that imprinted on our collective memory. And many of them are still rattling around in our hive mind. Remember who *originally* came to this land in the 1600s—boatloads of Puritans and Pilgrims. The Puritans were Anglicans who believed that their parent church was only partially reformed and needed a lot more work. The Pilgrims, on the other hand, thought Anglicanism was a lost cause. They felt they needed to establish a new, pure church. Both Puritans and Pilgrims (*Separatists*) believed European Christianity was a spiritual wasteland. They came *here* to escape it. In July of 1741 Jonathan Edwards preached a frightening sermon called "Sinners in the Hands of an Angry God"[8] to descendants of these people. What followed was largely unprecedented in church history: a lot of people made very public promises to be "better behaved" Christians. *Fear* dominated this movement. About fifty years later, a similar "Second Great Awakening" occurred, establishing a new precedent: *decision theology.*[9] This, along with a fear-driven faith, became the new model of Christianity in this land.

---

7. Of course it creates another problem: finding the church/pastor with the "right" list.

8. Edwards, "Sinners in the Hands of an Angry God."

9. This is a theological belief requiring individuals to make a *conscious decision* to

ONWARD CHRISTIAN SOLDIERS?

As the *norm*, decision theology formed certain expectations of all our people—even if they weren't particularly Christian themselves. It has stuck in our cultural expectation. "Born-again" spirituality took root three hundred years ago and even though it is a minority belief among American Christians it *still* largely defines our expectation of Christianity.[10]

This matters because most Americans have been unconsciously *primed* to expect religion to offer an emotional experience, amalgamated with an intellectual choice: something that they *decide* upon with an adult mind. As such it's become a consumer experience, with each individual in the driver's seat. Americans simply assume that a *true* religion will lead to decisions evoked because of an emotional encounter with God—usually through the dynamic preaching of a minister. Americans have an ingrained desire to "feel" saved in some way, which means they're looking for a crisis experience to define them religiously. "Salvation" has become something that's chosen after a pitch of some sort. And since mainline and Catholic churches aren't wired to produce this, many (most?) unaffiliated Americans unconsciously assume that these places aren't *really* "Christian." And many evangelical and fundamentalist preachers actually *say* as much from their pulpits.

Most surveys I've experienced reinforce this belief by asking questions like: "When were you 'born again'?"; "When did you 'accept Jesus as your personal savior'?"; "Does your church 'evangelize' by calling for people to 'repent of their sins'?" These questions (and hundreds just like them) bolster this uniquely American, and relatively modern, (*mis-*)understanding of Christianity. I would argue that each of these questions also reflects a profoundly flawed understanding of what's going on in the Bible.

That brings us to another hallmark of the modern American church: a sanctified *anti-intellectualism*.[11] Many people in the congregations that

---

"accept" Jesus into their heart as a personal savior (aka be "born again").

10. Roughly half of American Christians are descendants of mainline or Catholic churches that are not "decision oriented"; and as Pew recently observed, nearly a third of Americans don't identify as Christian or religious at all. That means only about 20 percent of Americans *actually embrace* "born again," or decision-based, theology. Yet this *minority* opinion dominates the American religious landscape today.

11. The term "anti-intellectualism" is not an implication that a person is not as smart as someone else. In fact some anti-intellectual people are extraordinarily bright. It means that a person will dismiss *evidence* that something he or she has believed in is incorrect. In Christian circles this is typically done because the individual prefers some tenet of "faith" to science. It is most often the fruit of a false dichotomy, rather than an actual conflict.

formed around decision theology further evolved to reject serious study of Scripture, the arts, psychology, philosophy, and science. At first this was mostly limited to fundamentalists of the late nineteenth and early twentieth centuries, and the Pentecostal movement birthing at about the same time. But after the Scopes Trial (1925)[12] a war was on for the brain of the church in the United States.

Fundamentalists have nearly always found a liberal arts education and the serious study of science "dangerous." For this reason they founded their own Bible colleges, suggesting that state schools and "liberal" Christian institutions like Harvard, Georgetown, Oberlin, Baylor, etc. were "at war" with genuine Christian values, and sought *undermine* the Christian faith. By the 1970s they were forming their own primary and secondary schools all over the country to offer shelter for "persecuted"[13] Christians. In the 1990s they began pushing homeschooling as the safest way to educate your kids (and keep your wife home where she belongs[14]). This helps to explain why the appointment of Betsy DeVos, a champion of many evangelical views, to head the US Department of Education was met with such praise from the Religious Right, and why she was so adamantly opposed by those on the left. The tie-breaking vote cast by Vice President Mike Pence, a vocal evangelical, will likely prove significant in cementing him as the darling of the evangelical voting bloc.

In the 1960s the church in the United States stood at a seminal crossroads. The older colleges and universities whose roots were solidly Christian had *acclimated* to the truth of science (evolution, psychology, sociology, cosmology, quantum mechanics, etc.). They were able to synthesize this knowledge with the Scriptures. Scholars like Helmut Thielicke,[15] H.

---

12. *State of Tennessee v. John Thomas Scopes*. John T. Scopes was accused of violating Tennessee's Butler Act for teaching human evolution in a state-funded school. William Jennings Bryan argued for the prosecution, while Clarence Darrow represented Scopes. The trial publicized the basics of the Fundamentalist–Modernist Controversy, which set modernists, who believed evolution could be consistent with religion, against fundamentalists, who taught (then and now) a literal reading of the Bible takes priority over everything else.

13. They posit that science and the liberal arts are tools of a "liberal conspiracy" thwarting Christianity.

14. We'll discuss "complementarianism," the evangelical/fundamentalist theory of male "headship," in chapter 7.

15. Thielicke, *Between Heaven and Earth*.

Richard Niebuhr,[16] Jacques Ellul,[17] Paul Tillich,[18] Harvey Cox,[19] and John A.T. Robinson[20] wrote challenging and insightful books and articles calling for Christians to live their faith more boldly, and with responsible attitudes toward science and culture. They urged the multitudes of progressive-minded disciples of Jesus to incarnate him differently from fundamentalists who were causing mainline Christians great embarrassment. A more moderate and intellectual Christianity could have prevailed, at least in large sections of the country, if the writings of these theologians had been embraced by more lay people. Sadly, that isn't what happened.

There's another aspect of moderate Christianity that is different from most of evangelicalism and fundamentalism, and it is a hot-button topic: the Civil Rights Movement of the 1960s. The stand of "liberal Christians" in solidarity with African-Americans in their struggle for racial equality lead to significant *progress* on that social front. It was also a sort of theological-social watershed moment. The descendants of those times, modern evangelical and fundamentalist Christianity on the one hand, and contemporary mainline and progressive Christianity on the other, still reflect the *ripples* of those polarizing times. Mainline churches have been far more inclusive of people of color than their conservative counterparts.

The next large-scale social movement, the women's movement of the 1970s and 80s, also demarcated along the same lines. Progressive Christians began ordaining women into ministry in the mid-twentieth century, while most conservative denominations still don't. In fact most evangelicals and fundamentalists ardently embrace "traditional" gender roles and teach *that* as the only valid scriptural position.[21]

The same goes for the paramount issue of *today*: homosexuality.[22] There are myriad social, political, and theological concerns that stream into *why* this is so, and I don't mean to minimize them. But the upshot is this: conservative church bodies are *conservative*—with *all* that brings with it. This fact may be troubling to some brothers and sisters in evangelical and fundamentalist Christianity, but it is undeniable that many people are

16. Niebuhr, *Christ and Culture.*
17. Ellul, *Meaning of the City.*
18. Tillich, *New Being.*
19. Cox, *Secular City.*
20. Robinson, *Honest to God.*
21. We will discuss this further in chapter 7.
22. We will examine this in greater detail in chapter 7 as well.

drawn *to* those churches for their societal conservatism, rather than any religious reason.

As proof I need only type two words: *Donald Trump*. Most evangelicals and fundamentalists are either proudly enamored of Trump (Jerry Falwell Jr.) despite his blatantly obvious un-Christlikeness; or they consciously prefer him to Hillary Clinton for intellectually and religiously *hazy* reasons. Over 80 percent of evangelicals and fundamentalists voted for Trump.[23] That is true despite the fact that he said countless unchristian things and has routinely acted in ways that are manifestly self-centered and narcissistic. A shockingly high number of evangelicals and fundamentalists, who despised Bill Clinton for his womanizing, actively support Trump *despite* his. And as more allegations were revealed following the inauguration Tony Perkins, head of the powerful Family Research Council, declared that they are giving Trump a "mulligan" for his sexual indiscretions.[24] That's obviously hypocritical. Let no one forget they impeached Bill Clinton and for his peccadillos. Many evangelicals have gone so far as to openly anoint Trump as "God's choice," and most are sticking to that.

There are reasons for this loyalty, and the intellectual gymnastics accompanying it. And those reasons aren't religious. We saw all this before. Evangelicals and fundamentalists have long claimed "family values" as their paramount issue. But in 2008 they glibly panned Barack Obama, who embodied the *best* image of those values in practice. They *also* universally condemned Mormonism as a "non-Christian cult" right up until 2012, when Mit Romney became the GOP nominee. It's all such a farce! The main source of right-wing opposition to left-leaning candidates is rooted in cultural and social *conservatism*, not politics, values, character, or even religion.[25]

Trump's ascendancy among evangelicals and fundamentalists is about *White privilege* more than anything else—including theology. His dangerous populism and divisive nationalism actually suits the evangelical and fundamentalist theological-political amalgam quite well. It also served to get a hardcore dominionist like Mike Pence a heartbeat away from the presidency. White evangelicals and fundamentalists *en masse* seem to have

23. Smith and Martinez, "How the Faithful Voted."

24. Burton, "Major Evangelical Leader Says Trump Gets a 'Mulligan.'"

25. The special election pitting Methodist Doug Jones against Evangelical Roy Moore only makes this more clear. White evangelicals and fundamentalists broke four to one for a man embroiled in a creepy teenage sex scandal, and who had twice been removed from the bench for focing his religious views on others in direct contradiction to US law.

no difficulty bartering away their "principles" to keep their *privilege*. As further evidence of this fact, consider that within a single week in mid-August 2017 nearly all of President Trump's business, industrial, technological, and humanities advisors resigned their posts in protest of the his inability to even *pretend* he's not supportive of White supremacy. A major group of Jewish rabbis cancelled their meeting with the president over the High Holy Days for the same reason. But only *one* member of his "Evangelical Advisory Board" quit his post in protest to his overt racism.[26] Secularist business leaders have more moral credibility in this country than evangelical megachurch pastors. To quote Mr. Trump: "SAD."

I recently had a lengthy conversation with my brother at a family holiday gathering. He is a typical example of what I'm talking about. Somehow the conversation turned to theology/church/faith. The air filled with electricity. You see, he's a solid, respectable deacon in a suburban, evangelical megachurch. He's a bright man: a process engineer for a large multinational firm that manufactures very expensive items for the militaries of the US/UK/NATO. He's a graduate of a top-tier evangelical college. And as I already noted, I'm a known faith-destroying heretic who's leading people straight to hell.[27]

In our discussion he said, off-handedly, "That's why Jesus had to die on the cross to pay for our sins." He was actually trying to find a point of agreement. He assumed that all Christians believe that God the Father demanded that his Son, Jesus: come to Earth, take our sins onto himself, and pay our death penalty sentence in our place. All because God arbitrarily decreed that death was the "punishment" for sin back when he was creating a literal Adam and Eve, in a literal Eden, 6,022[28] years ago. This is a cornerstone of evangelical decision theology. It's generally referred to as the "penal substitutionary atonement" theory, or PSA for short. It's also sometimes called the "Anselmic"[29] view of the atonement.

---

26. Pastor A. R. Bernard of the Christian Cultural Center in Brooklyn.

27. Not really, I just inserted that as dramatic hyperbole to make the story more interesting.

28. Most fundamentalists believe Adam and Eve were created in 4004 BCE + 2018.

29. Named after Anselm of Canterbury, an eleventh-century abbot who believed his view was a vast improvement on the far older "ransom theory," which was common among the church fathers (also called the *Christus Victor* view). PSA and Anselm's views are technically a bit different from each other, as are the "ransom theory" and *Christus Victor*, but for survey purposes they're close enough.

The main idea of the Penal Substitutionary Atonement Theory is that: God is totally holy; all mankind (since Adam and Eve ate the forbidden fruit) is born sinful; God demands death as the *penalty* to his offended holiness; in his goodness God sent Jesus to Earth and killed him as our *substitute*; so now we can go to heaven when we die! Personally, I think this notion makes God a bit of a monster at best, and more likely a deranged, bloodthirsty bastard. But one can't simply say that . . . like I did that afternoon. The room got very quiet and all my evangelical family members scooted a few feet away in anticipation of the lightning strike they were certain was about to burst from heaven to purge the world from such words.[30] But, when that failed to materialize, my brother hazarded to ask what *my views* were. I explained the broad points of *Christus Victor*[31] and suggested that the "ransom view" of the atonement makes a lot more sense to me scripturally[32]—and it has the added advantage of not making God out to be a psychopath. I explained that most of the early church fathers embraced some form of *Christus Victor*-ransom hybrid (if they bothered to say anything about *why* they believed Jesus needed to die).

What's *certain* is that the penal substitution view is less than a thousand years old, and wasn't particularly popular until after Thomas Aquinas codified it in his *Summa* in the late thirteenth century. In fact, very few people prior to 1400 would have ever imagined that *God killed his son in our place to pay a blood debt for our sins*! But my brother had never heard anything remotely like these *indisputable* facts. He explained that what "really happened" on the first day of church history (Acts 2) was that Peter conducted a revival meeting, ending with a traditional Baptist altar call. The organ played three verses of "Just as I Am," and three thousand people came to the front and invited Jesus into their hearts as their personal savior.[33] All

---

30. A bit more hyperbole.

31. An atonement theory that asserts our mythic first parents made humanity subject to death (the loss of divine life) and the devil during their fall in Eden, and that God, in order to redeem humanity, sent Christ to "ransom" them. In his ensuing resurrection Jesus broke open the doors of death and severed the devil's hold on all mankind.

32. Both the PSA and *Christus Victor* theories point to a God who loves humanity enough to send Jesus to into the flesh and to the cross to lead us back into a relationship with him. But in the *Christus Victor* theory Jesus enters into death to lead us out of its power, while in the PSA God kills Jesus (instead of us) to satisfy his own ruthless holiness. We will consider these ideas more fully in chapter 9.

33. A bit more dramatic hyperbole, mixed with loving sarcasm.

because those first believers knew that God killed Jesus in their place . . . so they could go to heaven after they die.

As you can imagine, it all ended very badly, with my brother slumped over in a chair pronouncing the inevitable: "Well, if you really believe all *this*, then I fear you're going to hell." It was all rather intense, and a bit unpleasant. My brother gathered up the kids and put in *WKRP in Cincinnati*'s "As God is my witness, I thought turkeys could fly" episode for comic relief—I think the irony of this totally eluded them![34]

34. And that's *not* added for dramatic hyperbole; it really ended that way.

3

The Breath of God

"My point . . . is not that those ancient people told literal stories
and we are now smart enough to take them symbolically,
but that they told them symbolically
and we are now dumb enough to take them literally.

—JOHN DOMINIC CROSSAN[1]

*great
quote!*

Books are the mirrors of the soul.

—VIRGINIA WOOLF[2]

OUR EVANGELICAL AND FUNDAMENTALIST brothers and sisters believe
Darwin was a dangerous man, and that the theory of evolution is a lie
straight from the pit of hell. They truly believe embracing evolution as
factual *denies* the Bible. Most can't tolerate any wavering on *this* point. In
their opinion any vacillating on this tenet of faith is tantamount to rejecting the *entire* Bible, and opening the floodgates to an outright rejection of
the existence of God. There are a lot of reasons why this particular point is
a *hub* their worldview rotates around. But summed up, they know that if
their view of Genesis as *literal history* fails, so does the primary rationale

1. Crossan, *Who Is Jesus?*, 79.
2. Woolf, *Between the Acts*, 144.

for their positions on a vast range of topics: from human sexuality and male superiority,[3] to "original sin" and a host of other beliefs associated with that theory, including decision theology. For this reason, denying a literal six-day creation is sufficient for most fundamentalists and many evangelicals to brand someone an "unbeliever."

Because of this it's equally a non-starter to attempt a reasoned conversation on the sciences of biology, geology, astronomy or, in most cases, archeology with most evangelicals and fundamentalists. Any overture on the evolutionary front will likely get you an invitation to take a trip to Ken Ham's "Creation Museum" and "Ark Encounter" near Williamstown, Kentucky. Fundamentalists and (most) evangelicals believe the first three chapters of Genesis *must* be interpreted as literally true—it's the *holy grail* of America's *anti-intellectual* faith. *It's also one of the main reasons the church has been losing so many of her youth!*

Many Americans have a *fatally narrow* knowledge of theology. They may know a good deal about a few things, but only from *one* point of view. When they encounter a *different point of view* they quickly reject it as "faith destroying." This kind of defensiveness and dismissiveness is a problem for the church of our day. It amounts to, "Don't bother me with the facts, my mind is made up." It's one thing *not* to know something. It's another to willfully *refuse to learn*. And that's where far too much of American evangelicalism and fundamentalism stubbornly remains!

Too many twenty-first-century Christians create what logicians call "false dichotomies" when they encounter new revelations that call for adjustments to older ways of thinking. They insist that the "new" knowledge creates dramatic either/or choices for people of faith: either the Bible is right and science (or whatever) is wrong, or vice versa. Many refuse to seek both/and scenarios. These Christians fail to comprehend that the way they *interpret* the Bible—their expectations of the Scriptures—is at least a part of the problem. This stubborn and willful ignorance is harming the church.

We must become more sophisticated as Christians. We need to know that nearly all the prominent early Christian bishops who discussed Genesis believed that it was a *mythic story*. Men with names like: Origen, Justin Martyr, Cyprian, Gregory of Nazianzus, Clement of Alexandria, and Augustine all believed that the creation account offered in Genesis should be understood as *allegory*—a story whose truth lay *behind* the text, not in

---

3. The word they use for male superiority is "complementarianism." We'll touch on it more extensively in chapter 7.

surface details. None of these great theologians believed God created the world in six literal days—because of that, all of them would be fired from any Bible college in America today, and from most evangelical universities. And *they* didn't have access to all the *science* on this topic we have—they came to this conclusion based solely on the way the story was presented *in the Bible*. Most pastors and bishops *closest* to the writing of the Bible believed stories like creation weren't intended to be taken at face value, that is, as literally true. They considered them to be symbolic accounts in which God is imparting deeper truths to humanity.

Fundamentalists and evangelicals are right about this: many kids go off to college and *learn* the *truth* in their first science class. They're convinced by the preponderance of science that the Earth is far older than six thousand years, and that humans have been evolving for hundreds of thousands of years. These young brothers and sisters quickly discover that they were taught a *sham* in church. Accordingly, many end up tossing the *whole faith* out as a pack of superstitious lies—all because their anti-intellectual parents and pastors grounded the veracity of their faith on an ignorant interpretation of the Genesis creation account. But it needn't be this way. The problem isn't with *evolutionary theory*. The problem is with a flawed understanding of what God is communicating to us in Genesis.

Too many American Christians have lost the ability to mine truth from "myth." And I know I just applied the frenetic word—*myth*—to the Bible. Which means (*to some*) that I just said it's a *fairy tale*, a made-up story written to entertain children at bedtime. But that's not what I *meant* to say! The word "myth" *literally* means no such thing. Myth is a respected and ancient form of literature that has been used for millennia to *teach* truth. Myths have been used to unite disparate groups of people into *communities* who see themselves as one. The tricky part is that it often employs images that are not *real* to do it.

Whole nations use myths. The King Arthur legends are formative for the British in this way. They speak to the values and codes of honor that make British people, British. As do the *Iliad* and *Odyssey* for the Greeks. Those Greek tales served their purpose so wonderfully that Maecenas commissioned Virgil to write the *Aeneid* to serve the same purpose for Rome. That myth simultaneously: offers legitimacy to Caesar Augustus and his political friends, establishes the value of "pietas" as uniquely honorable and "Roman," and depicts the Roman people as the heirs of the noble Greeks. Far from being "untrue," even though none of these stories happened in space and time, these myths were highly instrumental in making the British, Greeks, and Romans who they became. That's exactly what myths do! And it's exactly what the creation myth did for the Israelites—probably twice. This story came on the Israelite scene in some form as they were first uniting as a "nation" in the Promised Land, and again centuries later (when the original story was significantly reworked and altered) as the surviving "Jews" were coming back into Palestine after a couple generations in Babylonian captivity. It may even have been revisited and reworked in between these epic moments, as well.

In order to better illustrate this, let's shift gears for a second. If I say to you, "A man was going from Jerusalem to Jericho, and was attacked by a band of criminals along the way, who beat him severely, robbed him, and left him mostly dead on the side of the road . . ." you probably recognize what I'm referring to as the beginning of the "Good Samaritan" passage. So, did it ever *really* happen? The answer is not easy: things like that happened often enough that everyone hearing the story in the first century could easily imagine that part of the story happening literally. But the rest—the part about a priest, a Levite, and a Samaritan all coming along in short order; the part about the first two passing by without offering any aid and comfort, and the despised foreigner being the hero of the story—did that ever *really* occur? Almost certainly not. And no one suggests it did. It could have occurred in the realm of remote possibilities. But that's *not the point*! And everyone gets that. It's a story (parable) that teaches something profoundly *true*, without being literally *real*. That doesn't make Jesus a *liar* for telling the story. It's part of what made him such a compelling teacher. He communicated truth in powerful ways, some of which made use of unreal stories. That doesn't make the *truth* less true!

Emily Dickenson, a famously reclusive American poet of the mid-nineteenth century, penned this brilliant little poem:

> Tell all the truth but tell it slant—
> Success in Circuit lies
> Too bright for our infirm Delight
> The Truth's superb surprise
> As Lightning to the Children eased
> With explanation kind
> The Truth must dazzle gradually

Or every man be blind—[4]

"Tell the truth but tell it slant—" What does that mean? It sounds like *lying* to some people, but that's just the opposite of what this magnificent poet is actually suggesting. She knew that Truth, especially when it is expressed in "new" and unconventional facts, is difficult to accept when its just blurted out. It's a far better technique to gently lead people to discover new ideas slowly and almost by some sort of fortuitous accident. It's best to give people time and space to acclimate themselves to a new reality, to allow it to settle into their intellectual framework. Like in a story.

Stephen Crane does the same sort of thing in *The Red Badge of Courage*. Was there ever a real Henry Fleming? Did he really boast of his courage only to flee in his first real battle? Of course not! It's a story—but it's a *true story* even if *none of it actually happened.* Stephen Crane peels back the human psyche and shows us something of *ourselves.* We are made better people on so many levels as we wrestle with the events, feelings, and struggles of this American classic. That's what good novels, poetry, and short stories do. The same goes for plays, TV shows, movies, sculptures, paintings, and songs. They tell the truth, but they communicate it "slant"—in ways that give us space to gently introduce it into our *weltanschauung*: our world-life view. And that's a great way to educate people.

But most fundamentalist and evangelical Christians have difficulty applying the same standard to the Bible. They may give a pass to parables— they aren't intended to be viewed as "real." Some will even afford many of the Bible's poetry sections an exemption from the "literally real" litmus test. But don't mess around with Genesis. They insist that in the creation story there was: a real *talking snake*, a man whom God named "Dust Man,"[5] and one woman called "Source of Life,"[6] who were living in the "Garden of Delight,"[7] all of which transpired in one calendar *week*. Never mind that everything about the story screams "allegory." The very "names" are *archetypical.* Additionally, there's a poetic refrain running through the whole story, evoking a playwright marking the falling of a curtain and a *change of set*: "And there was evening and there was morning, the _____ day." Could anything say "change of scenery" louder? No one counts *days* by evoking

4. Dickinson. "Tell All the Truth."
5. Which is what "Adam" *literally* means.
6. The literal meaning of "Eve."
7. The literal translation of "Garden of Eden."

night/sleep to morning/wake cycles?[8] Nothing about this epic allegory calls for a *literal* interpretation. Quite the opposite!

And that's before you learn that the Genesis account of creation is strikingly similar to other creation myths from the region of the world cohabited by the children of Israel. The Egyptians have the Memphite tales, in which the god Ptah speaks creation into existence. And while there is no actual "creation" in the ancient Near Eastern *Atrahasis* epic, it discusses mankind and our relationship with the gods in strikingly similar ways to Genesis. Nearly all scholars (even some fundamentalists) agree that it is both older and likely provided direct source material for the Genesis account. There is also the Babylonian creation epic and the *Enuma Elish* creation epic, which also have strong parallels to Genesis—all predating it.

But there are some significant *differences* too. And that's what *should* grab our attention. After all, in the original context *that* is what would have jumped out to the readers/hearers of the tale. That's what marks them as *unique* from those around them. But too many American Christians don't want to dig into all that—they'd rather cling to an anti-intellectual falsehood and demand that the whole story be swallowed as literally true. And as they do, they totally miss the actual point of the mythic narrative! And they do great harm to the sensibilities of intelligent people, especially young Christians in high school and college.

The story of Genesis *isn't* about God creating everything in six solar days. The story is about God *intentionally* creating our visible world, and placing an object of *his love* at the center of it, as his *image bearer*: his special representative to rule and care for it in his place. The story is *actually* a lot more about his *breath*, which he placed in us, setting us apart from all the rest of creation. And our tragic rejection of his love communicated through the image of eating of the forbidden fruit in a pathetic effort to find a shortcut to godlike wisdom.

Let's pause and think about that *breath* detail. This "metanarrative"[9] of creation tells us of human formation at the initiative of God in Genesis 1:26–31. God then *breathes* his breath/spirit into the earliest people. This act results in them becoming *living beings*. God forms Adam (dust-man) out of the dirt and *then* breathes the breath of life into him. Consequently, he becomes *different* from the other animals (who also have *physical breath*

8. Besides hotels.

9. A story that offers a comprehensive rationale for human history, experience, and culture by offering an interpretation of universal truth and human values.

in them). Somehow God's spirit/breath is *exhaled* to us, and we become vastly *different*—superior to—all other life. God breathes into us (male and female) something of himself which altered humanity. It's not that we left off being physical and animal, it's that something was *added* to us so we are at once both animal and something *more*. Something divine.

This myth suggests that humanity began as clay and became the "image bearer" of God—which means we are his special *representatives*, tasked with doing his work in his name and by his authority. That happened when God breathed something of himself into us. Kissed us on the lips, so to speak. It is a special kind of blessing marked by intimate love. All creation is an expression of God and owes its whole existence to him, but mankind is different—special. We owe him the same debt of gratitude as everything else, and *more*! We are made in his image *more* than any other physical being. The creation story makes *that* clear.

By the way, the early church fathers—Origen, Justin Martyr, Cyprian, Gregory of Nazianzus, Clement of Alexandria and Augustine—all understood "day" to be a figurative reference of undetermined length. The first-century Jewish scholar Philo concurred. They frequently pointed to: "For a thousand years in your sight are like yesterday when it is past, or like a watch in the night";[10] and "But do not ignore this one fact, beloved, that with the Lord one day is like a thousand years, and a thousand years are like one day."[11] Both verses vastly expand time from God's point of view. In essence, they both "allegorize" two important words: "day" and "a thousand years."[12]

Nearly all Christian leaders closest to the writing of the New Testament preached and wrote about these kinds of stories as *allegory*: pregnant with powerful and deep meaning, but not *literally* true in every detail. None of them interpreted such stories as historical information or scientific truth. They referred to them as *spiritually true*—sources of divine certainty for mankind. They understood the power of story ("myth") to convey God's timeless and eternal truth to us. They relied on the power of mythic interpretation to *form* the nascent Christian communities they led.

10. Psalm 90:4.

11. 2 Peter 3:8.

12. The only other reference to a thousand years in the Bible is connected to the reign of Christ over his kingdom in Revelation 20. We'll spend some time with that in chapter 5.

God created humanity. And God placed his "breath" into us as a species at some point in our primordial past. He inhabits us in a way he doesn't inhabit any other life on Earth. Whether he especially guided the process of evolution, or simply found in our heritage something he could work with like no other form of life, doesn't matter—the Bible can be seen as embracing either possibility. What God did not do was make a literal couple (Adam and Eve), about six thousand years ago, in garden with a talking snake, over the course of precisely six days of twenty-four hours each. The mythic story of creation doesn't need to be viewed that way to hold it's meaning. Any insistence that it does reveals ignorance of scientific facts and of basic principles of interpreting literature. Refusing to learn this belies an arrogance bordering on obtuseness. And when this kind of ignorance drives people away from God, it is both inexcusable and it must be called out for what it is: false religiosity and idolatry.

Genesis is not the only place in Scripture that discusses the creative power of the breath/spirit of God in relation to humanity. Consider this story:

> The hand of the Lord was upon me, and he brought me out in the Spirit of the Lord and set me down in the middle of the valley; it was full of bones. And he led me around among them, and behold, there were very many on the surface of the valley, and behold, they were very dry. And he said to me, "Son of man, can these bones live?" And I answered, "O Lord God, you know." Then he said to me, "Prophesy over these bones, and say to them, O dry bones, hear the word of the Lord. Thus says the Lord God to these bones: Behold, I will cause breath to enter you, and you shall live. And I will lay sinews upon you, and will cause flesh to come upon you, and cover you with skin, and put breath in you, and you shall live, and you shall know that I am the Lord." So I prophesied as I was commanded. And as I prophesied, there was a sound, and behold, a rattling, and the bones came together, bone to its bone. And I looked, and behold, there were sinews on them, and flesh had come upon them, and skin had covered them. But there was no breath in them. Then he said to me, "Prophesy to the breath; prophesy, son of man, and say to the breath, Thus says the Lord God: Come from the four winds, O breath, and breathe on these slain, that they may live." So I prophesied as he commanded me, and the breath came into them, and they lived and stood on their feet, an exceedingly great army.[13]

13. Ezekiel 37:1–10.

This is one of many odd visions that the prophet Ezekiel experiences during his ministry. God brings Ezekiel to a desolate valley full of skeletal remains. Ezekiel's vision draws on the creation imagery of Genesis to show us the greatness of God's power in creating and recreating life.

Ezekiel's Valley is full of *death*, our age-old enemy . . . bones of those who were killed in some battle of old. God invites Ezekiel to join him in creative—*re-creative*—work. Ezekiel breathes out God's words over the remains, and the bones come together and flesh covers them: a field of human bodies lay "sleeping." This is a state like Adam after he is formed of clay, but *before* the *life-breath* of God is exhaled into him. Ezekiel speaks over these shells; he calls to the *breath* that they may really live! And they jump to life! It is a fascinating story. While the original message is focused on the nation of Israel, it's a *spiritual reality* that is further reified in the church. What was true for the *nation* of Israel is also true for the church as the spiritual kingdom of God. The Holy Spirit was breathed into us in a new way at Pentecost.

This brings me to one of the most difficult things to talk honestly about within the modern American church: *abortion*. Most pastors who've served in a congregation for any period of time have spoken with at least one grieving woman wrestling with guilt because she's had an abortion.[14] Sometimes it occurred a week ago . . . sometimes half a century past, but her shame often remains quite raw. And, tragically, the church is often a central part of her struggle.

No one celebrates abortion! No one! No one wants his or her daughter to grow up and have one. No one. No one wants to learn that his or her mother or grandmother had one. No one. I believe it's important to emphatically establish this because there are people in our country who claim that large swaths of "liberal" America view abortion as some sort of perverse "sacrament." Some suggest that pro-choice people[15] are haters of procreation. If you've listened to Rush Limbaugh, Glen Beck, or Sean Hannity you've heard just this sort of thing stated *repeatedly*. Take for example this discourse: "Abortion is the highest sacrament in the Church of Liberalism.

14. And this is just as true for fundamentalists and evangelicals as anyone else. Most surveys reveal that women from such churches have abortions at about the same levels as other groups based on their percentage of the overall population. See Jerman, Jones, and Onda, "Characteristics of US Abortion Patients in 2014 and Changes since 2008."

15. Who they often denigrate with appellations like "pro-abortionist" or even "baby-killer."

The killing of children is considered even holier and more sacred to its disciples than gay marriage or genital mutilation. Like the primitive pagan cultures before them, liberalism looks upon the sacred rite of child sacrifice with a deep reverence. The liberal has a cult-like, religious devotion to the sacrament of infanticide. Liberals will venerate it for the same reason Catholics venerate the Eucharist and Muslims the Koran—because it is the centerpiece of their worship, the core, the soul of the thing."[16]

And it's an outrageous lie! No one celebrates an abortion . . . or sixty million abortions. No one. But abortions happen. They have always happened, and they *will* always happen. Anyone with a heart grieves this reality. And anyone with a brain contemplates how to address the *underlying problems* within this nation—*the richest nation the Earth has ever seen*—that have driven so many women to seek this solution to pregnancy. But for millions of women an abortion is the *least terrible* solution available. And so they have one. And generally they *survive* because it is *regulated* and reasonably safe.

A less-well-known fact is that abortions occur far *less often* when birth control is readily available and affordable; that probably ought to be self-evident. And because this is also an undeniable fact, I would think both pro-life groups and right-wing political extremists like Mr. Limbaugh would join in calling for increased *funding* for programs that provide contraceptives. That approach is far more "cost effective," and has the added benefit of dramatically reducing abortion rates. But the religious and political Right often prefer to "slut-shame" women who have sex outside marriage . . . or *in* an abusive one, or who are raped,[17] or victimized by incest, or whose lives are threatened by a dangerous pregnancy, or who are carrying a defective fetus, or *whatever*, instead. They do this for many reasons and most are *political*, not moral or religious.

Sometimes anti-abortion activists, like David Green, one of the owners of Hobby Lobby, actually take their anti-intellectualism to another level by claiming that birth control pills "cause abortions."[18] Birth control pills do not cause abortions, and anyone who's read the scientific literature on the

16. Walsh, "Attention, Pro-Aborts."

17. Let us not forget that in August of 2012, Rep. Todd Akin (R-MO) publically stated that women don't get pregnant when they're *really* raped—a falsehood commonly believed on the far right.

18. They do this to give the appearance of *moral legitimacy* to their resistance to providing birth control to their employees—the truth is they are attempting to impose their religiously motivated morality (opposition to sex outside marriage) on others—which is a separate issue.

THE BREATH OF GOD

subject knows it. Dr Dennis Sullivan, director of the bioethics center at my very conservative alma mater, Cedarville University, has called for honesty on this point. Sullivan reviewed emergency contraceptive research for a peer-reviewed article in *Ethics & Medicine* in 2012. He found "no evidence" that the emergency conception pill "Plan B" causes abortions. He writes, "Our claims of conscience should be based on scientific fact, and we should be willing to change our claims if facts change."[19] The science surrounding birth control pills is crystal clear: they *do not* cause abortions. And while the supreme court ruled in Hobby Lobby's favor, they did so by stating that Green's fact-resistant, anti-intellectual faith is guaranteed under the First Amendment. How embarrassing! Denying the science on the subject is *not* the best way to present Christ's kingdom. It makes followers of Jesus look hateful and stupid. It makes us look controlling, puritanical and unsympathetic. These are things Jesus never was!

But that's not the topic before us—abortion is. Is abortion the murder of a human being? *That's the question.* In Jewish law and tradition a fetus is not typically considered a human being until it's *delivered* from the mother's womb and takes its first breath. Most Jewish rabbis and faith communities affirm this understanding based on their interpretation of the Torah. Even in orthodox Jewish halakah law, abortion is *not* forbidden. This is vitally important because *most* of the passages cited by evangelicals and fundamentalists against abortion are found in the Old Testament. So it's logical to consider what the historic understanding of the people who created, and first used, those holy writings has been. In fact there is no New Testament passage that deals directly with abortion at all.

To better understand this issue we need to know that modern Protestant opposition to abortion did not crystalize around numerous, clear Scripture passages. Nor did it form around attitudes of the early church, the Reformation era, or during the "Great Awakenings." It's very contemporary. As recently as 1973, the Rev. Dr. Wallie Criswell,[20] who served as president of the Southern Baptist Convention, said: "I have always felt that it was only after a child was born and had a life separate from its mother that it became an individual person, and it has always, therefore, seemed to me that what is best for the mother and for the future should be allowed."[21] He

19. Dennis Sullivan, as cited by Moon, "Does Plan B Cause Abortion."

20. Editor of the *Criswell Study Bible* (1979), popular in evangelical and fundamentalist circles.

21. Criswell, as quoted by Flynn, *Lawful Abuse*, 33.

was hardly alone. A couple of prominent professors at Dallas Theological Seminary (DTS), the flagship of evangelicalism, weighed in similarly on the abortion question in the early 1970s. Bruce Waltke stated emphatically: "God does not regard the fetus as a soul, no matter how far the gestation has progressed."[22] There is nothing ambiguous about that opinion! He based his position on the Old Testament, which he believes teaches "life begins at birth." He also argues that Assyrian law "prescribed death by torture in cases of procured abortions. The fact that God did not set forth a similar law becomes even more significant . . . Mosaic Code is normally more extensive and severe than other codes."[23] And fellow DTS professor Norman Geisler concurred, stating: "The embryo is not fully human—it is an undeveloped person."[24]

In 1968 *Christianity Today* cohosted an important gathering of prominent evangelicals and members of the Christian Medical Society. They discussed both abortion and birth control from a scriptural perspective. They created a statement titled "A Protestant Affirmation on the Control of Human Reproduction." It states: "Whether the performance of an induced abortion is sinful we are not agreed." These leaders could not agree whether abortion was sinful in the eyes of God. This is hardly a ringing endorsement, but miles from where they are today! But they went further: "But about the necessity of it and the permissibility of [abortion] under certain circumstances we are in accord."[25] In other words, they could not agree whether God viewed abortion as sin, but they could agree that it was an *essential option* for women to have access to abortion. And not just in cases where the life of the mother was in jeopardy, they stipulated that "family welfare, and social responsibility" were also valid reasons for abortion. They blessed abortions for "family planning." This attitude parallels the traditional attitude of Jews on this topic, as well as the historic position of mainline churches.

Statements like these caused little stir in the 1970s. Articles covering this topic from *various* points of view were regularly carried in evangelical magazines. Professors at leading evangelical seminaries were free to express *divergent* opinions based on their understandings of Scripture. That's because fundamentalists and evangelicals of that time had no great difficulty

22. Waltke, "Contraception and Abortion."
23. Waltke, "Contraception and Abortion."
24. Geisler, *Ethics: Alternatives and Issues*, 211.
25. Stripe et al, "Protestant Affirmation on the Control of Human Reproduction."

with abortion. Abortion was not on their radar as a "sin" before the late 1970s. What led to their change of attitude is unimportant for my purposes, except to note that it wasn't the discovery of some Bible passage that had been previously overlooked or misunderstood. It was *politics*. And it was a brilliant political move, serving to amalgamate power for right-wing religious leaders and politicians. We'll get into that in chapter 4. They managed to "define" the issue, by inventing the idea that "life begins at conception." This novel idea afforded them the right to claim the moral high ground against their opponents, and rally their followers around the most moral of causes. But the issue is far less settled from an actual scriptural standpoint.

We need to briefly survey the pertinent texts on the issue—don't worry, there aren't many! The most common passages used by Christians in condemnation of abortion are: "Now the word of the Lord came to me saying, 'Before I formed you in the womb I knew you, and before you were born I consecrated you; I appointed you a prophet to the nations.'"[26] Then from Psalm 139:13–16: "For it was you who formed my inward parts; you knit me together in my mother's womb. I praise you, for I am fearfully and wonderfully made. Wonderful are your works; that I know very well. My frame was not hidden from you, when I was being made in secret, intricately woven in the depths of the Earth. Your eyes beheld my unformed substance.[27] In your book were written all the days that were formed for me, when none of them as yet existed." And the only New Testament passage to be regularly employed in this debate: "In those days Mary set out and went with haste to a Judean town in the hill country, where she entered the house of Zechariah and greeted Elizabeth. When Elizabeth heard Mary's greeting, the child leaped in her womb. And Elizabeth was filled with the Holy Spirit."[28]

The most obvious problem with using the Jeremiah and Luke passages as broad-spectrum anti-abortion texts is that both passages are laser focused on *individual* men, or rather babies who later grow into men. Neither text has any notion of speaking universally of *all* fetuses. That's a serious problem to applying them across the board. Nothing else in the context is true for all others. There is absolutely no reason to suggest God's "knowledge" of Jeremiah implies he had a soul at that time. And unborn John "leaping" in the womb as proof of a soul *in utero* stretches credulity. In

26. Jeremiah 1:4–5.
27. The Hebrew word here is *golem*.
28. Luke 1:39–41.

fact the Spirit in this passage is upon *Elizabeth*, not pre-born John, which actually reinforces the traditional view that the fetus is an extension of its mother until "delivered."

Psalm 139 is less restricted in this sense, and for that reason most anti-abortionists go to it before the others. However, the main punch of this text is actually a *reverse whammy* for those who suggest unborn fetuses have souls. This passage actually suggests the *opposite*! The key to understanding this passage is found in a Hebrew word in verse sixteen: *golem*. The legend of the golem is an ancient one, but, *long story short*, a golem was a clay figure that became animated through secret knowledge. Golems[29] were used in Hebrew folklore to perform very dangerous tasks that require a human-like ability and knowledge, like mining or other equally perilous jobs. According to ancient Jewish folklore, people would make golems and send them to do that sort of work, because they were *not* actually human!

In Psalm 139 the pertinent word *golem* is translated into English variously:

- "my substance, yet being unperfect"[30]—KJV;
- "unformed body"—NIV;
- "unformed substance"—ESV, NASB, NRSV;
- "fetus"—GOD's WORD translation; and
- "imperfect being"—Douay-Rheims.

The term is a *challenging* idea to get across in a word or two. "Soulless android" just doesn't cut it when you're talking about a mother's unborn baby! But *that's* what the word *literally* means. What's unformed, imperfect, and incomplete in this fetus is a *soul*—the breath of God.

Here are a couple passages that tend to speak against a fetus having a soul: "Why did you bring me forth from the womb? Would that I had died before any eye had seen me, and were as though I had not been, carried from the womb to the grave";[31] and, "And I thought the dead, who have already died, more fortunate than the living, who are still alive; but better

---

29. Quickie Hebrew lesson: words are made plural by adding an "m" in Hebrew. So we have one seraph and five seraphim, or one cherub and eight cherubim. Golem seems to be like the English word "deer": it's form can be either singular or plural in Hebrew—though in Anglicized form we add an "s" to make the word plural.

30. Spellcheck doesn't like it, but that's the word the KJV uses.

31. Job 10:18–19.

than both is the one who has not yet been, and has not seen the evil deeds that are done under the sun."[32] These passages share a dark wish to have been aborted or miscarried—to have *never been*. This is far from "proof." But Job and Qoheleth[33] both suggest that babies who are never born simply cease to be—or, more accurately, *never were*. If we desire to be "Israel," people who *wrestle* with God, we should strive to discover what the Scriptures *actually* say on this or any other topic, and allow that to guide us as we form our opinions.

Two final passages: "When people who are fighting injure a pregnant woman so that there is a miscarriage, and yet no further harm follows, the one responsible shall be fined what the woman's husband demands, paying as much as the judges determine. If any harm follows, then you shall give life for life, eye for eye, tooth for tooth, hand for hand, foot for foot, burn for burn, wound for wound, stripe for stripe."[34] In this passage the Bible offers a scenario where two people are fighting, and somehow cause lethal injury to a pregnant woman. Exodus says they are to be put to death. However, the scenario states, if they only cause her to miscarry and don't cause the woman to die, they are only fined for the injury to the *woman*. This seems to indicate that God does not consider the fetus as fully human.

Also consider these words: "If any man's wife goes astray and is unfaithful to him, if a man has had intercourse with her but it is hidden from her husband, so that she is undetected though she has defiled herself, and there is no witness against her since she was not caught in the act. . . . In his own hand the priest shall have the water of bitterness that brings the curse. Then the priest shall make her take an oath, saying, 'If no man has lain with you, if you have not turned aside to uncleanness while under your husband's authority, be immune to this water of bitterness that brings the curse. But if you have gone astray while under your husband's authority, if you have defiled yourself and some man other than your husband has had intercourse with you,'—let the priest make the woman take the oath of the curse and say to the woman—'the Lord make you an execration and an oath among your people, when the Lord makes your uterus drop, your womb discharge; now may this water that brings the curse enter your bowels and make your womb discharge, your uterus drop!'"[35]

---

32. Ecclesiastes 4:2–3.
33. The assembler or preacher of Ecclesiastes.
34. Exodus 21:22–25.
35. Numbers 5:12–13, 18–22.

In this text God prescribes what is commonly referred to as a "trial by ordeal." In this scenario if a husband *suspects* his wife has been unfaithful, but he has no actual proof, he is permitted to bring her to the priests, who will give her an abortifacient of some sort. If she miscarries, then his suspicions are vindicated, and no illegitimate DNA enters his lineage. If she and her pregnancy survive, then she is deemed innocent. The sexism latent in this ancient text may be odious to us, but the point for us is that God seems to turn a blind eye toward causing a miscarriage, and actually *prescribes an abortion* in Numbers 5. These facts have to be mixed into our understanding of this topic to truly honor God's revealed will.

I want to repeat that I don't believe anyone celebrates abortion. I also believe it would be much more honoring to God if we spent our efforts addressing the most prevalent factors causing women to feel their least horrible option is to seek one. Evangelicals were on that path in the late 1960s. In the November 1968 issue of *Christianity Today* evangelicals appealed to the role of birth control as the key solution to abortion in our nation. More recently, Rachel Held Evans puts it this way: "Instead of focusing all of our efforts on making 'supply' [abortion] illegal, perhaps we should work on decreasing demand. And instead of pretending like this is just an issue of women's rights, perhaps we should acknowledge the very real and very troubling moral questions surrounding a voluntarily terminated pregnancy."[36] This makes all kinds of sense, but current fundamentalist and evangelical leaders seem to be fixated on *denying* both options, fearing that distributing condoms and birth control pills will open the floodgates to premarital sex. Such prudish and naïve attitudes are fruit of anti-intellectualism, revealing that controlling *other people's* actions are the true goals of these groups.

Nothing about abortion is easy. But simply wishing it away doesn't work. And shaming it away is actually quite destructive. Women have abortions; they always have, and until we mitigate the actual underlying causes, they always will. Adding unwarranted stigma to a woman who's had one only diminishes any hope that she'll ever find wholeness in this life. And that fact runs counter to what followers of Jesus should be most concerned with. Compassion demands we address this issue with grace. God wants us to find these women and bless them with his love. They often feel like failures. They don't need more hostility and abuse—most have had more of that than we can imagine. They need love, inclusion, and acceptance for

36. Evans. "Why Progressive Christians Should Care about Abortion."

who they are: *women who have made the most difficult decision any woman can face.*

We were discussing *breath* a few pages back. One more thing about breath: the church is supposed to follow Jesus—we're supposed to be like him. *We're supposed to be a breath of fresh air to the world,* like he was. But far too many who claim the name "Christian" are bags of hot and *angry* air instead! I hear echoes of Ezekiel in the words of Jesus in the Gospel of John the night of the resurrection in the closed room. He greets the assembled disciples with "peace." That is the point, after all! That's what the angels said on the night of his birth. In the Fourth Gospel we have another *breath* moment—a Holy Spirit moment: "And when he had said this, he breathed on them and said to them, 'Receive the Holy Spirit. If you forgive the sins of any, they are forgiven them; if you withhold forgiveness from any, it is withheld.'"[37] He exhales the Holy Spirit on them—he said so himself. And there is a special gift that accompanies this bestowing of the Holy Breath of God: the *power to actually forgive sins.* God is breathing into his people the potential for them to embrace their divine calling. "Dustman" can be so much more—the image-bearer of God who dwells within creation to bless it as God would. That's what followers of Jesus are supposed to be doing. We're supposed to walk around breathing forgiveness, *restoration,* and *God's favor* on people. We've been given a "ministry of reconciliation."[38]

All through the Gospels we see Jesus meet people where they are, as they are, and *breathe life into them.* He takes time to dine with whores, Pharisees, traitors,[39] demoniacs, and loads of regular folks. In the end he enters into "death," the death humanity brought onto itself through its self-centeredness and hubris. He does this so he can bring us to "life." Releasing our "death-dealing" by dying to our *self-righteous* bent is the first step in discipleship. That's part of what Jesus means when he says, "Take up [your] cross daily and follow me."[40] Jesus looks at us in our *messed-up-ness,* and instead of shouting, protesting, and demanding that we *change our ways,* he lays down his life. He meets us at the very sum of our fears, so he can take his life up again, and share that eternal/resurrection life with us! That's the model he gives us to follow.[41]

---

37. John 20:22–23.

38. 2 Corinthians 5:18.

39. Which is how tax collectors were viewed.

40. Luke 9:23.

41. 1 Peter 2:21, also see John 13:15 and Luke 9:23.

During his earthly ministry, Jesus was asked to identify the "spirit" of the Old Testament Scriptures by summarizing the Torah with a single law. This practice provided a glimpse of the "prism" through which any rabbi filtered the Scriptures, and reveals a great deal about his attitude toward God. This type of question was common in Jesus' day, and every rabbi needed to be prepared to answer it. It provided an opportunity for rabbis to assess each other's basic *hermeneutic*—the way each approached God's word. In that sense there was no wrong answer, as long as he cited something in the Hebrew Scriptures. There was no right answer either, and rabbis commonly argued with one another about the basic hermeneutic that others used. Popular answers often referred to circumcision, the laws of sacrifice, rules surrounding the Sabbath, and the holiness of God. Jesus opts to paraphrase a portion of the prayer many Jews recite twice a day: the "Shema Yisrael." Jesus blends two passages[42] into a single thought. We find this in Matthew 22:35–40: "A lawyer asked him a question to test him. 'Teacher, which commandment in the law is the greatest?' He said to him, 'You shall love the Lord your God with all your heart, and with all your soul, and with all your mind. This is the greatest and first commandment. And a second is like it: You shall love your neighbor as yourself.' On these two commandments hang all the law and the prophets." Jesus places love at the heart of his theological understanding. In Matthew's Gospel he says: "In everything do to others as you would have them do to you; for this is the law and the prophets."[43] A similar idea is found in the Fourth Gospel: "I give you a new commandment, that you love one another. Just as I have loved you, you also should love one another. By this everyone will know that you are my disciples, if you have love for one another."[44]

As the church wrestles with moral issues, these passages should form our starting point. God invites us to enter his kingdom as sons and daughters and join in working together to make life *just* for everyone. The Bible is the light that shines into the darkness of human selfishness to lead us all in that direction—and the life of Jesus is the apex of that vision. Followers of Jesus need to get more serious about living as he did, embracing the values of grace, mercy, and forgiveness he embodied. We have been called to take up a cross—to die to self-righteousness and "superiority." We need to *resurrect* with Jesus by killing *fear* and *legalism* and embracing the

---

42. Deuteronomy 6:4–5 and Leviticus 19:18.

43. Matthew 7:12.

44. John 13:34–35.

self-sacrificial love of our Master. We must to learn to rest in the One who has made us God's children in baptism and who feeds us at the altar. We need to start risking a lot more and sacrificing of ourselves to _bless_ those whom Jesus would have us bless—which is everyone! It is only in this way that we reclaim the soul (breath) of the church!

4

Politics, Jesus' Style

It is easier to make fidelity to God about believing the absurd,
than to make it about what the Bible says it is about,
namely radical compassion, love, giving, and self-sacrifice.

—JAMES F. McGRATH[1]

"Something's rotten in the state of Denmark,"

—SHAKESPEARE[2]

A SECOND MAJOR TENET[3] shared by most evangelical and fundamentalist believers, separating them from more moderate, mainline Christians, is their concept of Jesus' kingdom. Most mainline Christians are taught to think of Christ's kingdom as a *present reality* existing now on Earth (though imperfectly). We find support for this attitude in passages like: "God put this power to work in Christ when he raised him from the dead and seated him at his right hand in the heavenly places, far above all rule and authority and power and dominion, and above every name that is named, not only in this age but also in the age to come. And he has put all things under his

1. McGrath. "Swing By and Pick Up the Llamas."
2. Shakespeare, *Hamlet, Prince of Denmark*, 1134.
3. The first being their much more *literalistic* handling of Scripture.

feet and has made him the head over all things for the church, which is his body, the fullness of him who fills all in all";[4] and: "May you be made strong with all the strength that comes from his glorious power, and may you be prepared to endure everything with patience, while joyfully giving thanks to the Father, who has enabled you to share in the inheritance of the saints in the light. He has rescued us from the power of darkness and transferred us into the kingdom of his beloved Son, in whom we have redemption, the forgiveness of sins."[5] It is a mainline hallmark to consider the kingdom of God as already inaugurated, though not yet revealed in its entirety.

Most fundamentalists and evangelicals, conversely, envision the kingdom primarily as a *future* reality one enters after death—"heaven." For devotees of rapture theology,[6] it's perceived as occurring only after Jesus returns to Earth following a great battle called "Armageddon." These brothers and sisters believe Jesus will return to Earth in the future with the sole purpose of establishing a *literal* thousand-year reign centered in Jerusalem. This difference drives the whole focus of either group, and since they are different, everything built upon them is different.

Mainline Christianity is far more deeply rooted in the *present* than our evangelical and fundamentalist counterparts. Our faith is largely expressed by working to make *this life* better for those who live with want, need, inequity, and injustice. Seeking to correct these discrepancies is at the heart of how we believe we participate in building Jesus' kingdom. We work in this life to make his kingdom more visible in this world, something Paul referred to as "birth pains,"[7] knowing that task will never be complete until Jesus returns at the end of time. This return is called the "parousia"[8] or the "second coming." And while most Christians believe in *that*, we hold significant differences from most evangelicals and fundamentalists concerning what we think it will look like. We'll discuss some of those differences more specifically in chapter 5.

For its part, evangelical and fundamentalist Christianity tends to be considerably more *future* focused. It is also more "dualistic" or "Neoplatonic" than progressive Christianity—that means most evangelicals and

4. Ephesians 1:20–23.

5. Colossians 1:11–14.

6. Technically named "dispensational premillennialism." We will discuss it more fully in chapter 5.

7. Romans 8:22.

8. In Greek it literally means "presence," "arrival," or even "official visit."

fundamentalists are distrustful of physical reality as innately perverse. There are myriad reasons for their disdain of the physical body, which they sometimes even refer to as the "prison house of the soul." Most of these reasons are historical and philosophical and beyond our scope.[9] The practical result of their belief system is that fundamentalists and evangelicals diligently strive to get as many people *out* of this fallen world and into the next. To use their terminology, they're driven to "get people saved, so they'll go to heaven when they die." They long for the day when they believe Christ will bring his kingdom from heaven to Earth—after the rapture, tribulation, and Armageddon.[10] They are looking for Jesus to return to Earth to establish his kingdom quite *literally* in Jerusalem. The upshot of their belief system is this life becomes something of a puzzle for evangelicals and fundamentalists because the only purpose for life in the present (in their view) is to prepare for the one to come.

This rupture between the present and Jesus' *future* reign has fostered a modern reincarnation of the nineteenth-century doctrine called "manifest destiny." The modern iteration is called "dominionism."[11] It was popularized beginning in the 1970s by R. J. Rushdooney and C. Peter Wagner, with support from David Barton, D. James Kennedy, Francis Shaffer, Jerry Falwell, Tony Perkins, Paul Wayrich, and James Dobson. It is wildly popular among many fundamentalist and evangelical Christians—many of whom have never heard the term. Some variant of it is the dominant political view of several leading GOP politicians, including: Ted Cruz, Rand Paul, Rick Perry, Michelle Bachmann, Sarah Palin, Tom Coburn, George Allen, Jim Talent, Sam Brownback, Wm. "Jerry" Boykin, Jim DeMint, and Mike Pence, to name a few of the most prominent. Judge Roy Moore would also fit into this camp.

In essence, they desire to make America a modern *theocracy*—a country ruled by (*their* interpretation of) the Bible. They want to compel *all* Americans to follow biblical laws, as they determine are appropriate. To justify the imposition of religious rules on everyone, they posit that America was founded as a "Christian nation."[12] They further contend that the United

9. Brian McLaren outlines them brilliantly in chapter 4 of his book *A New Kind of Christianity*.

10. Concepts we'll discuss in more detail in the next chapter.

11. It is also sometimes called "Christian nationalism," "kingdom now," and "Christian reconstructionism." It is not a monolithic set of beliefs, but most varieties share several key elements.

12. Something that is demonstrably false, but an essential mythology to their

States Constitution was virtually inspired by God and is a reflection of his will for humanity. And while not all premillennialists[13] are dominionists,[14] dominionists nearly always espouse dispensational premillennialism.

Dominionists apply biblical commands directly to *America* whether the individual people involved are Christian or not. They view the United States as a modern correlation to the Old Testament *nation* of Israel. Of course, they pick and choose which laws to enforce. Homosexuality remains an "abomination" to most.[15] Accordingly, they believe God expects America to outlaw homosexual behavior for all people. But most are OK with people eating shrimp and bacon, and wearing blended fabrics—all things that the Old Testament forbids in much clearer terms.

There's no general consensus of which biblical laws dominionists desire to impose and which are no longer in effect. For example, Ted Cruz routinely calls for the defunding of Planned Parenthood as a main tenet of his brand. Pat Robertson's brand led him to say he would only bring Christians and Jews into the government, during his 1988 presidential campaign. Many Dominionists deny manmade climate change because they believe God holds absolute control over the weather. They don't believe human activity *could* cause global warming, because that would make man greater than God![16]

What Dominionists *do* share is the belief that God wants Christians to permeate government on all levels and pass laws and regulations that require outward conformity to what they perceive to be God's moral code. The fight over defunding Planned Parenthood is a perfect example, though it's actually a "Trojan horse" argument. Dominionists claim they want to outlaw abortion, or at least prevent taxpayer-funded abortion (which is *already* forbidden under the Hyde Amendment). But the *real* issue is premarital sex. Dominionists oppose all sexual activity outside marriage, even for people who aren't Christians. *Contraception* is their biggest enemy on this front—and so it must go. As we discussed in chapter 3, they oppose abortion based on their belief that a fertilized egg is as fully human as you

---

rationale.

13. Proponents of rapture theology.

14. Christians who desire to impose "biblical" morality on all Americans.

15. The Bible never addresses monogamous, consensual homosexual relations. Something we'll look at in chapter 7.

16. This is another example of "faith" compelling many evangelicals and fundamentalists to dismiss settled science (facts) because of their anti-intellectual interpretation of Scripture.

or me, but their actual (hidden) agenda is to criminalize all sex outside marriage.[17]

Dominionism began to emerge within the GOP in the late 1970s and was a *fait accompli* by the middle of Ronald Reagan's administration. As an Xer,[18] I was young as this occurred, but Millennials[19] have never seen anything different. It contributes to their frustration with the church in America, a phenomena which is aptly discussed in numerous books.[20] Millions of American Christians, young and old, male and female, gay and straight, reject this political view because it fails to reflect *Jesus* as they know him from the Gospels. They realize Dominionists are striving to create a different political kingdom from the one Christ outlines. Evangelicals and fundamentalists seem to ignore many of Jesus' instructions, and reach back to the ethno-political kingdom of Israel for their inspiration. They transfer God's expectations for the nation of Israel to America. It is wrong, and millions of more moderate followers of Jesus see that . . . and the numbers are growing each day.

Jesus spells out his agenda for *living* our faith in an impressive sermon in the early pages of Matthew's Gospel. Understanding what kingdom Jesus offers and what kingdom we're called to build with him is vital! Matthew was written in part to explain this. Matthew's Gospel first appeared in the region north of Jerusalem during a time of intense persecution when many first- and second-generation Christians were dying without seeing any hints of a literal, physical kingdom form under the leadership of a returned Jesus. Disappointment prevailed in the psyches of many Christian communities of that time. This Gospel reminds its readers not to be surprised by that experience. Jesus had announced a kingdom, not of power and might like Rome, but of grace and forgiveness—one of the cross. These facts pave the way for the "Discourse of the Kingdom"—the sermon that explains what Jesus' kingdom is supposed to look like, and how his followers are supposed to incarnate the reality of his reign in this world: "Blessed are the poor in spirit, for theirs is the kingdom of heaven. Blessed are those who mourn, for they will be comforted. Blessed are the meek, for they will inherit the earth. Blessed are those who hunger and thirst for righteousness, for they

17. See Hawkins, interview on *The Joy Reid Show*.

18. The age cohort born between 1964 and 1984.

19. The age cohort born between 1985 and 2005.

20. See Kimball, *They Like Jesus but Not the Church*; McKinley, *Jesus in the Margins*; Gibbs, *ChurchNext*; and Bolz-Webber, *Pastorix*.

will be filled. Blessed are the merciful, for they will receive mercy. Blessed are the pure in heart, for they will see God. Blessed are the peacemakers, for they will be called children of God. Blessed are those who are persecuted for righteousness' sake, for theirs is the kingdom of heaven. Blessed are you when people revile you and persecute you and utter all kinds of evil against you falsely on my account. Rejoice and be glad, for your reward is great in heaven, for in the same way they persecuted the prophets who were before you."[21] These ten statements, known collectively as the Beatitudes, are a new Ten Commandments for a new age. That's not to suggest the old Ten Commandments are obsolete, but rather that they are fulfilled in *love*—as Jesus said numerous times.[22]

The Beatitudes were written into a particular context: the first-century Roman Empire. They were first heard in historically Jewish lands. We know how "peace" was kept, and how the people lived—their hopes and fears—in this era. The famed *Pax Romana*, or "Peace of Rome," was a "peace" that came through force, violence, and repressive law. "Justice" was swift, firm, and inflexible . . . unless you were *rich*. There was a well-understood notion of what a kingdom looked like to most first-century Jews living in Palestine: the Rome they lived under (a hated enemy), and a *romanticized* version of King David's reign. Many first-century Jews simply plugged Jesus into their *long-established expectations*: Jesus as King David 2.0, a slightly more perfect king who would lead national Israel into renewed glory, make tons of bread from just a couple of loaves, heal all their sick, and even occasionally raise their dead!

The kingdom Jesus describes bears scant resemblance to either of those. His kingdom is: inclusive, not exclusive; positive, growing out of the Old Testament Torah, which paved the way for it; reconciliatory, built through radical grace, mercy, and forgiveness; decidedly *egalitarian*—embracing men/women, Jews/Gentiles, and rich/poor;[23] and a community—a family—that works together to bless the whole. Jesus presents a kingdom of the cross, not a kingdom of power and glory. He calls for personal suffering and sacrifice to construct this kingdom: "Take up [your] cross and follow me."[24] Along with the cross, he makes the basin and the towel symbols of

21. Matthew 5:3–12.
22. See Matthew 22:35–40 and John 13:34–5 as examples.
23. Galatians 3:28.
24. Matthew 16:24/Luke 9:23.

his movement.[25] Personal sacrifice, suffering to bless others, and service of all have always been the motto and symbols for followers of Jesus.

However, many first-century people—like many modern folks—desire a kingdom where *we* are ensconced on thrones, and others (or even God himself) serve us. This proclivity explains most of the major problems within the church over the ages. We trade the kingdom of the cross for the latest version of a kingdom of glory. This error is at the heart of evangelical and fundamentalist church (and dispensational premillennialism too).

There are a few more important kingdom issues presented in Matthew 5. Jesus tells us that we are supposed to be *salt* and *light* in the world. Salt and light serve no purpose by themselves. They only become valuable as they interact with things which are *not* salt or light. The idea that the salt or light was supposed to *transform* everything they came into contact with into yet more salt or light is a confused metaphor. Salt blesses meat it is rubbed onto—but leaves it as meat. Light reveals the path; it doesn't convert everything it shines on into more light. This may seem quite obvious, but a large segment of the church seems to have missed this fact. They act as if they believe a Christian's main job is to make everyone else *believe*, and especially *act*, as they do. They mean well, but their notion of Jesus' kingdom is flawed, and their misunderstanding leads to a host of other problems. They believe that building the kingdom of Christ necessarily requires some sort of altar call where people will be confronted with their need to *consciously* and *intentionally* join Jesus' team. This is not what John the Baptist and Jesus meant when they called people to "Repent, for the kingdom of God is at hand."[26] This confusion has grown out of a modern democratic milieu where we vote for our "king," not one where a king arrives and makes his claim irrespective of his would-be subjects' individual desires.

After the salt and light metaphors, Jesus pauses in his extended sermon to explain that he has no intention of eliminating the Law or the Prophets as he transfers their obligation to his church. Then he offers six small discourses that we call the "Antitheses." By that we mean Jesus takes six familiar laws or rules from Old Testament Judaism and he turns each on its ear. He *radically reinterprets* Moses and other established truisms. Each of these "Antitheses" includes a phrase like this: "You have heard that it was said ___x___, but I say to you ___y___." It's difficult for us to comprehend how radical this was! Jesus is flying in the face of all that Israel had believed

25. Matthew 26:14–39; Luke 22:24–27; and John 13:1–17.
26. Matthew 3:2 and 4:17.

about herself as a people for over a millennia. He was tinkering with what they had always been told God demanded of his people. He imposed his personal (and untried) understanding in place of rules that had come to them from Moses. That's likely why Matthew presents Jesus as an uber-Moses in the second chapter of his Gospel—the otherwise unreported story of another mad king killing all Jewish baby boys. Talk about hutzpah!

The priests and Pharisees saw what Jesus was doing, and as a result, regarded him as dangerous. They felt he was threatening their security by changing the rules that had kept them in the marginal (at least) grace of their vindictive and unpredictable God.[27] In fact, Jesus was trying to free people from *that* specific attitude, and introduce them to a *long-suffering* and *loving* God instead. Jesus insists his followers respect *every* human's dignity. He begins by saying: "You have heard that it was said to those of ancient times, 'You shall not murder' . . . but I say to you," if you're angry, insult or cuss at someone, you'll be liable to "the hell[28] of fire."[29] In other words, Jesus values our personal relationships with others ahead of religious piety! To illustrate his point, he offers some ridiculous examples: anger will get you executed; cussing will result in a trial in Israel's supreme court; and calling a person "a fool" will get you sentenced to time in the city dump where miscarriages and the corpses of criminals were burned with other biological refuse (Gehenna).[30] These examples are *not intended* to be seen as *literal* outcomes! They are "hyperbolic"—literary exaggerations to draw people in. The apex comes when he suggests that someone with a strained human relationship should leave the temple if he were there to make a sacrifice to God. He should seek restoration with his estranged brother first, and then pick things up with God!

 Second, Jesus addresses the practice of "dehumanizing" someone for personal pleasure. He says: "You have heard that it was said, 'You shall not commit adultery.' But I say to you," objectifying women for your own

27. The kind that sends hurricanes or tornadoes to destroy whole cities, or fire to burn down wicked people's houses, or make you sick because you don't tithe.

28. We're going to discuss Jesus' view of "hell" in chapter 9. It's not the same as ours.

29. Matthew 5:21–26. Obviously, I paraphrased the end portion to shorten it, and added the italics for emphasis, which I'll do in the following five passages as well.

30. The "Gehenna of fire" was a literal place on Earth in the time of Jesus. It was a garbage dump outside Jerusalem. And, odd as it may sound, people would literally go there and stay for a period of time as a public display of their sorrow for something rotten they'd done. It was never an "eternal" thing, though some people would spend several months in this kind of public contrition.

pleasure amounts to *dehumanizing* others who are also made in the image of God. Jesus values all people equally, and so should we.

Third, while Jesus seems to simply forbid divorce (except for infidelity), his point is actually far more nuanced. He says: "It was also said, 'Whoever divorces his wife, let him give her a certificate of divorce.' But I say to you," selfishly casting a wife aside to hook up with a younger woman is sin.[32] In the first century it was not uncommon for a man with means to divorce his wife so that he could replace her with a "younger model." Jesus speaks into *that* context: one in which *only men* could initiate divorce.[33] Three rabbis influenced the moral attitudes of most Jews in terms of divorce in the first century:

- Rabbi Shammai taught that a man could divorce his wife only if she were unfaithful—that was actually a *kindness* because he could demand her *execution*.

- Rabbi Hillel suggested a husband could divorce his wife if she failed to be a *good* wife, especially if she burned his meals.

- Rabbi Akiba actually said a man could divorce his wife if he found a woman who was *prettier* than his current wife!—the original "Arm Candy Clause."

When Jesus weighs in on this topic, these three men and their rules were fully in play in the minds of his listeners. We have to take that into account.

It's also important to understand that in Jesus' day an unmarried woman (divorced or widowed) was nearly always reduced to abject poverty. There were exceptions, but they were rare. The only feasible way for most women to survive after such a divorce (especially of the latter two types) was to prostitute themselves in one way or another, because their hopes of a second marriage were essentially nil. This teaching is aimed at a culture that was so sexist that women were essentially seen as lacking value beyond bearing children, cooking, and providing sex. Divorce is actually secondary in this text to the underlying problem. In the new kingdom Jesus is outlining women are to be regarded as *equal* in value to men.

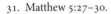

31. Matthew 5:27–30.

32. Matthew 5:31–32.

33. In Mark 10:12, where Jesus speaks of women divorcing their husbands, he is actually making up a radically new option for Jews. That passage actually follows the same thoughts as here.

✳∖∖ Fourth, Jesus tackles the issue of deceptive business practices. He says: "Again you have heard that it was said to those of ancient times, 'You shall not swear falsely' . . . but I say to you," deceiving people with fine print and tricky word games is wrong.[34] The main point here is Jesus opposes getting a "good deal" by deceiving, tricking, or otherwise exploiting people. We've all been there—we've made a deal with some salesman or neighbor, only to discover later that the item we bought wasn't what we had been led to believe. Of course, sometimes this happens accidently. But more often a smooth wheeler-dealer has snookered us. Jesus denounces trickery that advantages one person at the expense of another. He returns to this topic in Matthew 23.

✳∖ The fifth topic is one which many Christians, especially within evangelicalism and fundamentalism, have completely forgotten—or which they choose to ignore. This is especially noticeable as they beat the tom-tom of American militarism. How often have we heard a Christian pastor or politician denounce an American enemy in Jesus' name, calling down God's wrath for a slight (real or imagined)? Senator Rick Santorum, one-time darling of evangelicals, famously quipped, "Let's load up our bombers and bomb [ISIS] back to the seventh century."[35]

The Rev. Dr. Gary Cass, an ordained pastor in the very conservative Presbyterian Church in America,[36] published an article in the September 2014 issue of *Charisma* titled, "Why I'm Absolutely Islamaphobic."[37] Among other things he calls for the immediate deportation of all Muslims from the United States and the *eradication* of all Muslims worldwide—genocide! Cass has also written, "Why We Cannot Coexist" and "You Can't Be a Christian If You Don't Own a Gun." Cass *literally* calls for the *extermination* of over one billion people—based solely on their religion. Yet, ironically, he has been lauded as "pro-life" by the fundamentalist and evangelical community. He isn't some obscure nut; he's *well known* within right-wing political and religious circles. He holds masters and doctorate degrees from Westminster Theological Seminary in California. He has received the Salt and Light Award from evangelical champion D. James Kennedy and serves as the executive director of Kennedy's *Center for Reclaiming America for Christ*. This group has been cited as one of the top ten "pro-family" organi-

---

34. Matthew 5:33–37.

35. Santorum, speech, February 27, 2015.

36. Not to be confused with the mainline Presbyterian Church in the USA (PCUSA).

37. Cass, "Why I'm Absolutely Islamophobic."

zations in America. Yet he believes violence can usher in peace for Christians—as most American evangelicals and fundamentalists do.

Yet Jesus expressly taught the opposite! In Matthew 5:38–42 he says: "You have heard that it was said, 'An eye for an eye and a tooth for a tooth.' But I say to you," don't violently resist evil doers; when struck, turn the other cheek, and when compelled to carry a Roman soldier's gear for one mile (a law every Jew hated) I say, willingly carry it two miles.[38] Most Christians know Jesus said these things, but the American evangelical/fundamentalist movement has practically dismissed them out of hand. I can't tell you how many evangelical and fundamentalist acquaintances I've heard evoke Exodus 21:24, where the Torah first gives us the "eye for an eye" notion of proportional retaliation/justice. Then they promptly jettison the "proportional" part—like both Santorum and Cass have publically done. It apparently never occurs to them that Jesus set this Old Testament rule aside in favor of radical *mercy* and *forgiveness*. He tells us that his kingdom will be built on the spine of sacrificial grace, not violence and retribution. *That's* what "Take up [your] cross and follow me" means. It doesn't mean we should, like fourth-century Rome, paint crosses onto our shields, and go kick ass for Jesus . . . which, by the way, *is* what actually created Islam in the first place!

Finally, Jesus says: "You have heard that it was said, 'You shall love your neighbor and hate your enemy.' But I say to you love your enemies and pray for those who persecute you."[39] Far from lashing out at people of whom we disapprove, Jesus says we are to bless them! He demands that we love our enemies—and not in some *contrived*, "tough love" way. Love them by blessing them and praying for them (meaning, asking God to bless them too). He points out that God sends sunshine and rain to people who hate him just as much as those who serve him.[40]

The "Sermon on the Mount" forms the *essential teaching*—the *ethic*— of the *kingdom of God*. Jesus was speaking mainly to first-century Jews living under Roman rule in the Promised Land—living virtually as slaves in

---

38. I find it incredible that some Christians use their faith to refuse service to gays, Muslims, or African-Americans based on *their* "religious" rights. Jesus would command a Christian cake baker to bake two cakes for anyone "oppressing" them! Modern American Christians who claim such exceptions have no idea what real oppression is, and no idea what following Jesus actually looks like. They are spoiled, whining children, not faithful disciples.

39. Matthew 5:43–48.

40. So much for Pat Roberson's notions of God wrathfully smiting wrongdoers!

the land God had given to his people centuries before. The Holy Land was occupied by Gentile forces. The high priest was a puppet of Rome, as was the king (Herod). The real power was imperial Rome, and everyone knew it. As far as worldly kingdoms go, Rome is a model. But not for Jesus. He didn't say, "I'll establish a kingdom like Rome . . . except I'll add in a bit more morality"—which wouldn't have been setting the bar very high! But for most American fundamentalists and evangelicals, that's exactly what they want. *Except they substitute* America *for Rome.* Far too many Christians believe that America is a "Christian nation." They cheer every time we go off to solve some perceived problem with our tremendous military might. They claim we're "putting the fear of God" in our enemies as we drop bombs and deliver death and destruction from halfway around the globe. But it's not true!

Jesus showed us what the kingdom of God looks like. And it doesn't look anything like "Shock and Awe."[41] *God isn't interested in putting his fear in anyone*—he's far more interested in *putting his love into them.* Consider:

> Pursue peace with everyone, and the holiness without which no one will see the Lord. See to it that no one fails to obtain the grace of God; that no root of bitterness springs up and causes trouble, and through it many become defiled. See to it that no one becomes like Esau, an immoral and godless person, who sold his birthright for a single meal. . . . You have not come to something that can be touched, a blazing fire, and darkness, and gloom, and a tempest, and the sound of a trumpet, and a voice whose words made the hearers beg that not another word be spoken to them . . . you have come to Mount Zion and to the city of the living God, the heavenly Jerusalem, and to innumerable angels in festal gathering, and to the assembly of the firstborn who are enrolled in heaven, and to God the judge of all, and to the spirits of the righteous made perfect, and to Jesus, the mediator of a new covenant, and to the sprinkled blood that speaks a better word than the blood of Abel.[42]

The "meal" many American evangelicals and fundamentalists are willing to sell their "birthright" for is safety—security bought through militarism. This *secondary* god is the *protector* of America's main god: materialism. As a people we worship our greed and violence more than we realize. We trade away the words of Jesus and reach back to Moses to justify ourselves. But

41. The use of overwhelming military power and spectacular displays of force to paralyze an enemy's psyche—also the nickname of the US bombing of Iraq in 2003.

42. Hebrews 12:14–24.

the Messiah, our true king, has made it abundantly clear that this is a seriously flawed choice.

Just after this lesson, Jesus offers us a family prayer: "Our Father in heaven, hallowed be your name. Your kingdom come. Your will be done, on Earth as it is in heaven. Give us this day our daily bread. And forgive us our debts, as we also have forgiven our debtors. And do not bring us to the time of trial, but rescue us from the evil one."[43] The "Lord's Prayer" is actually a *political* prayer when you consider it in context. It's political in the sense that it's all about us getting onboard with *Jesus' agenda* and building *his* kingdom, rather than trying to *sprinkle him into ours*! Jesus continues his "Sermon on the Mount" with some more very *un-American* things: he tells us not to live accumulating things on Earth; he speaks about the filters of our eyes; and he explains that we can't serve two masters (especially God and money). But that hasn't stopped many American Christians from trying!

Then Jesus addresses anxiety. It makes you wonder if we would choose to stop chasing the illusive "American dream" of materialism and personal self-fulfillment, maybe, just maybe, we would find we need a lot less _____ to be happy. Preeminent psychologist Abraham Maslow developed a landmark "hierarchy of needs," which suggests we'd be more likely to find happiness ("actualization") if we spend more time and effort tending to the needs and problems of those around us. Jesus pointed that out two thousand years ago, too, in the feeding of the five thousand.[44] Jesus saw the crowds, and though he and the twelve were hungry and tired, Jesus directed them to look at the crowd—to really see and care for them. He asked the Twelve, "Where are we going to find food to feed all these people?" I suspect the "*non-actualized*" twelve all thought, "Why is that *our* problem?" What could be a more American attitude? We know how this story develops: Jesus takes a boy's lunch, multiplies it to fully satisfy all those people, then they collect baskets full of leftovers. One of the main points of the story is that we get more out of serving than we do out of taking! What could be more politically liberal? It makes you wonder if Jesus was some sort of a socialist.

So, WWJD[45] politically? If Matthew 5–6 hasn't made it clear, Jesus gives us the *Golden Rule*: "In everything do to others as you would have

43. Matthew 6:9–13.

44. Matthew 14:13–21.

45. What would Jesus do?

them do to you; for this is the law and the prophets."[46] We also know how he would treat his enemies, the poor, women, LGBTQ people, minorities, and people who hold differing religious views—including the Pharisees! "Shock and Awe" were not out of the realm of Jesus' possibilities. But that's not his way. Intimidation, violence, and bullying cannot be the go-to response of Christians to solve our problems. Jesus would never do it. Nor should we.

For the first three hundred years of Christian history all pastors and bishops were in agreement with this—and many of them were *really* persecuted. I don't mean they were made to bake cakes for gay couples. They were thrown to lions, lit on fire to illumine gardens, crucified, and other equally unpleasant things. But they took Jesus' words seriously. And their testimony to Christ "turned the world upside down." They cared for orphans during famine; they didn't cheat on their wives (as a rule), they didn't rape children and slaves, and they didn't cheat people in business deals. Christians were known to be pacifists who cared deeply for the poor and disabled. They welcomed strangers and cared for old women. All this was true right up until Constantine managed to seduce key church leaders and merge the failing Roman state with the church—naming Christianity as the "official" religion of the empire.

It probably seemed like a coup for many Christians at the time. But it was a sinister trap. Following this merger of church and state, much of Jesus' teaching was cast out of the new "Christendom." Crosses were painted on the Roman army's shields, and the rest is history. Instead of looking like Jesus, Christianity looked like . . . well, it looked a lot like it looks today, which is tragic. And that raises the question: Do we reflect the "Sermon on the Mount"?

The church needs to become reacquainted with Jesus. Instead of acting entitled and compelling others to live like we think they should, we need to start spending a lot more time striving to live like Jesus told *us* to live—and that never includes making people do what we want. Instead of walking (or blogging) around complaining that we are being oppressed, we need to start seeking to bless others in body, soul, and mind. And we need to be doing it sacrificially. Maybe then we'll find that we're a lot more attractive to young people. But if not, at least we can be sure that we're doing what Jesus actually asked us to do—build his kingdom, his way!

46. Matthew 7:12.

5

A Discussion of the Rapture

The mass of men lead lives of quiet desperation.
What is called resignation is confirmed desperation . . .
But it is a characteristic of wisdom not to do desperate things.

—HENRY DAVID THOREAU[1]

It is not the task of Christianity to provide easy answers to every question,
but to make us progressively aware of a mystery.
God is not so much the object of our knowledge as the cause of our wonder.

—KALLISTOS WARE[2]

Remember Jimmy Webb's question asked in the Fifth Dimension's 1967 hit, "Would you like to ride in my beautiful balloon?"[3] In this sunshine pop hit from half a century ago, Webb suggests that the world is a nicer place when viewed from someplace disconnected high above. He envisions love and companionship in his "beautiful balloon." He lifts us above all the chaos, hatred, and injustice—not to mention violence, exploitation, and the

1. Thoreau. *Walden*, 7.
2. Ware, *Orthodox Way*, 14.
3. Webb, *Would You Like to Ride in My Beautiful Balloon?*.

meaninglessness of life. It's *escapism*, at its best. And people loved it then, and still do today!

The "rapture," as it's presented by Hal Lindsey and LaHaye/Jenkins, is strikingly similar. Christians float away to heaven with Jesus where they watch as God pours out his *wrath* on those left on Earth. Heaven in general, and the rapture in particular, have become a theological *narcotic* for the *self-obsessed* who seek a front row seat to view divine vengeance visited on "the other," while they are exempted. It's spiritual escapism bordering on prurience. The rapture theory serves to provide an escape from humanity's brutality toward itself and the destruction of our natural world. It offers cover for people who know the shibboleth, while demanding little in the way of actual effort.

According to proponents, Jesus has a lot of unfinished business in this world. They teach that he must return to fulfill a literal Davidic-style reign centered in Jerusalem. In rapture theology the present is a great *parenthesis* in human history called the "Church Age," or the "Age of Grace." Since the Jews largely rejected Jesus as their Messiah, according to this theory, God put his dealings with them on hold and began working with a replacement people—the church, which became predominantly Gentile within two generations of Jesus.

For Lindsey and LaHaye that means God hasn't actually fulfilled his Old Testament promises.[4] So they're waiting for a reboot of human history. The dominant eschatological view of evangelicals and fundamentalists is modern version of an old heresy: "chiliasm."[5] They renamed their version "dispensational premillennialism." This theory suggests that God has dealt with the world according to six rulebooks (and one more to come). They divide human history in epochs ("dispensations") bound by various covenants, during which God's "plan of salvation" changes. In effect, the rules were different for Methuselah than they were for Jeremiah; God dealt with Cain under plan two and David under plan five. The specifics don't matter for us—but we find ourselves in the sixth such epoch: the Church Age. For the moment (the theory holds) God is paying attention to Gentiles. And that's good news for us. But we're still essentially just the half-time show, until Jesus returns and assumes King David's throne in Jerusalem for a literal thousand year reign (plan seven). Then, he will be mostly focused on the Jews again, and those who readopt the temple sacrificial system,

4. Another example of literalism gone amok.
5. Deriving from the Greek word *chilia*, meaning "thousand."

which is why rebuilding a temple in Jerusalem is vital to evangelicals and fundamentalists.[6]

This is how the our era will conclude and the final epoch will roll out according to rapture theology:[7] Jesus will come *toward* the Earth, but stop short (in the air); an angel will sound a trumpet, which *only* Christians will hear;[8] and all *Christians* (living and dead) will be caught up[9] and be taken to heaven to be judged. *Meanwhile*, back on Earth, God the Father begins pouring out his *wrath*: called the "tribulation." It will last for the *same* seven years. During which: The "Beast" will come to power with the "False Prophet"; a literal, God-hating, "one-world" government will be formed under the "Antichrist."[10] God will open seals on a scroll, pour out bowls and vials, more trumpets will sound, and horrible *wrath* will rain down on all people. The famed four horsemen of the Apocalypse play a part in this chaos. In a solitary sign of good will toward humanity, God will send two human prophets to explain his fury, and announce that he'll love them and stop his vengeful wrath if they change their ways.[11] At the end of the seven years the Antichrist will gather an army to war with God, and Jesus will return all the way to Earth with his angels and the saints. They will touch down on the Mount of Olives and Jesus will kill the Beast's army: the blood spilled will be two hundred miles long and four to five feet deep.[12] After this battle Jesus will cast the devil into a "bottomless pit," and will judge the survivors, some of whom will be willing to accept him as their king. They alone will enter a literal thousand-year kingdom ("millennium"). The

6. Hebrews 7:27 is simply ignored.

7. In its modern incarnation this theory owes a lot to the nineteenth-century John N. Darby, founder of the "Exclusive Brethren," and C. I. Scofield of the early twentieth century. John Walvoord of Dallas Seminary lent his credibility to the theory in the mid-twentieth century, leading up to Lindsey and LaHaye's novels. It has never been a prominent theory among the mainline churches, Roman Catholics, or the Orthodox, which comprise 80 percent of the church.

8. Nowhere else in all the Bible is there a secret trumpet that only some hear; in fact the point of trumpets is that they are so loud that *everyone* can hear them!

9. This is where the word "rapture" actually comes from—the Latin *rapiemur*, or *rapio*, meaning "to catch up." Popular books speak of pilotless planes crashing to the ground, driverless cars careening all over, and pagan mothers wondering where their Christian children disappeared to, etc.

10. The book of Revelation never actually uses the term "Antichrist."

11. Which is pretty much the textbook definition of abuse and conditional love!

12. Is it any wonder that, despite Jesus' clear teaching of non-violence, proponents of the rapture view are quick to anoint US wars as God sanctioned?

rest are sent to the "Lake of Fire" to be burned alive for temporal eternity. Jesus will rule over this small group, which will grow exponentially through procreation and low mortality. At the end Jesus will release the devil from the "abyss," and he will raise a mob to attempt to kill Jesus and set up their own kingdom (*again*).[13] This, of course, fails, and they too are thrown into the Lake of Fire. The survivors enter into eternity. So ends human history.

There are more details: myriad gory things happen. But, boiled down, Christians get to watch as God smites the world's people, big time—and Americans seem eager to want to watch a good smiting! So, like "Up, Up and Away," most evangelicals and fundamentalists enthusiastically antici-pate a version of the future that presents them *rising above* the mayhem and having a front-row seat to view the wicked get theirs, while they party with Jesus. It all sounds ominously like those who seek a different version of heaven complete with five dozen virgins—*fundamentalisms* seem to share a perverse desire to watch all people who believe differently from them eradicated by God, while they get to look on like voyeurs. It's sinister and sadistic . . . not to mention unbiblical.

I realize that those who embrace this theory cite passages, and have glitzy charts full of Bible references, and arrows, and graphics, to simplify all the moving parts. However, all through church history, the vast majority of pastors and theologians have soundly rejected this horrible hack job on the Bible. It's built on bad exegesis of the Hebrew and Greek (and English). And it's rooted in *vengeance*, something Jesus never exhibited in his earthly ministry.[14]

Several times throughout Jesus' ministry he said, "The kingdom of God is at hand." Luke 17:20–25 puts it this way:

> Once Jesus was asked by the Pharisees when the kingdom of God was coming, and he answered, "The kingdom of God is not com-ing with things that can be observed; nor will they say, Look, here it is! or There it is! For, in fact, the kingdom of God is within you."

13. Why people will hate this perfect reign of Christ is never explained.

14. *All right*, there was that one moment in the temple when he ran the moneychang-ers out with a whip and flipped over a couple tables, but those guys were in cahoots with corrupt priests and collectively they were fleecing the people and placing temple rites out of reach of the common man—exactly what the temple was never supposed to be! They were effectively extorting people for God's forgiveness, and no one was killed. In fact, there's some question if anyone was actually whipped. The Bible never actually says Jesus *used* the whip. That story is the *one* rare exception to Jesus meek and gracious, building a kingdom based on the ideals of the Sermon on the Mount.

> Then he said to the disciples, "The days are coming when you will
> long to see one of the days of the Son of Man, and you will not see
> it. They will say to you, Look there! or Look here! Do not go, do
> not set off in pursuit. For as the lightning flashes and lights up the
> sky from one side to the other, so will the Son of Man be in his
> day. But first he must endure much suffering and be rejected by
> this generation."

Based on Jesus' own words you might expect that the modern dispensa-
tional/rapture theory would be laughable. But most evangelicals, and *really*
all fundamentalists, prefer to embrace a *Left Behind* style of theology where
they get to watch God roast, skewer, and vaporize unbelievers—by which
they mean those who haven't accepted him into their hearts in the way
they believe one must. Many almost gleefully recount how they will get to
watch the four dreadful horsemen savage the population of the Earth with
violence, disease, death, and famine. It fits in with their revivalistic, "Sinners in the Hands of an Angry God" theology perfectly.

Not only do they transform Jesus into a vindictive ogre, they fail to
comprehend that the horrible things depicted in Revelation *have been going
on* for nearly two thousand years and counting[15] . . . which is what Jesus actually meant! And that's really at the heart of the problem. Most evangelicals
have a wrathful image of God; their God is *scary*! They also seem to have a
general lack of understanding of *human history*. They apparently can't see
that the Black Death, which killed somewhere between seventy-five and
two hundred million people in Europe from 1346 to 1353,[16] is apocalyptic! Likely 95 percent of Native Americans[17] died of diseases inadvertently
introduced to this land by the Puritans, Pilgrims, and Georgetown settlers.
The Spanish flu pandemic of 1918 infected five hundred million people (or
one third of the world population), killing as many as one hundred million
worldwide. One and a half million Irish perished in the mid-nineteenth-
century potato blight. Ten million died in 1932–33 in a Russian famine,
and twenty-five million in 1958–62 of famine in China. Yet dispensational
premillennialists don't see these numbers as having any connection to the
dreadful events recounted in Revelation.

Neither do they see deaths from war and violence over the last two
millennia as addressed in the last book of the New Testament: over a million

---

15. Many of them have been happening since the dawn of human history.

16. Easily 30–60 percent of Europe's population at the time.

17. Probably about twenty million people.

people in the siege of Jerusalem in 73 CE; forty million in China from 184 to 280 CE in the Three Kingdoms' War; seventy million in the Mongol War, which raged in the thirteenth and fourteenth centuries; six million in Napoléon's early nineteenth-century wars; and eighty-five million people as a result of World War II. And there are the untold numbers who died at the hands of "The Shining Path" in Peru, the Mujahedeen/ Taliban, ISIL, or Boko Haram; Apartheid, Pol Pot, the Mexican Drug Wars; victims in Aleppo, Darfur, Bosnia, South Sudan. Evangelicals and fundamentalists view none of that carnage as depicted in Revelation.

They don't see fulfillment of John the Divine's words in the disruption and destruction of our oceans,[18] toxic algae, red tide, global climate change, Chernobyl, Fukushima, weird cancers and other maladies once so rare now becoming increasingly (and alarmingly) common—and yet rapture proponents are still *waiting* to see the four horsemen *begin* their ride!

This obtuseness is more fruit of anti-intellectualism—an alarming lack of awareness of basic science and history. And it gives rise to another important point: too many people calling themselves "Christian" feel little *empathy*, and no *responsibility*, for those suffering most because of war, famine, disease, and exploitation. Far too many evangelicals and fundamentalists glibly say, "Close our borders and keep the 'illegals'/refugees out!"[19] It verges on sociopathic. It certainly doesn't reflect the compassion that so often moves Jesus throughout the Gospels. The callousness of those who fail to have any solidarity with the masses of displaced, abused, exploited, and starving humans doesn't remotely reflect *Jesus' attitude* toward people.

There's one more thing that is "part and parcel" of modern dispensational premillennialism: they have an unwavering and uncritical support for the modern Israeli state. Have you ever wondered why so many preachers and politicians profess resolute support of the Israelis, no matter what they do? Some Christians cite Genesis 12:1–3 as the basis of this blind support of Israel: "Now the Lord said to Abram, 'Go from your country and your kindred and your father's house to the land that I will show you. I will make of you a great nation, and I will bless you, and make your name great, so that you will be a blessing. I will bless those who bless you, and the one who curses you I will curse; and in you all the families of the Earth shall be

18. The WWF released a report in 2014 stating that there has been a decline of 39 percent of marine and mammalian populations from 1970 to 2010, and an incredible decrease of 76 percent for fresh water species. See Thompson, "Global Wildlife Populations Have Fallen by Half."

19. The UN believes that there were over sixty million refugees worldwide in 2016.

blessed.'" On the surface it might appear to pertain, but it doesn't for several reasons.

This passage was *fulfilled* in Jesus, the one in whom all the nations of the world *have been* blessed. Also, the New Testament expands the role of Jesus. He's not just king of Israel, but God's anointed king of *all creation*. The church is presented as his subversive kingdom in the world. Repeatedly Paul says God has no more (or less) love and concern for Israel than any other ethnicity, tribe, language, or nation. God looks at all people as *equally* important. However since Israel's formation as a country on May 14, 1948, the United States, influenced by evangelicals and fundamentalists, has bent over backwards to arm, defend, and support it.

A more biblically faithful view concerning the end times, one embraced by most of the early fathers and reformers, is to understand that Jesus *established his kingdom while he was here on Earth*. It was never intended to be a physical kingdom. It is one formed around the values expressed in the Beatitudes[20] and Golden Rule.[21] It's one in which service to the poor and sick and visiting and relieving the distress of widows, orphans, and prisoners are key values.[22] The "world system" is frequently *represented* in the Bible by figures like Pharaoh, Caesar (or King Herod), and ultimately the Beast. The way of life embraced by people who fail to order their lives around the values promoted by God are presented as being in *opposition* to his kingdom. That's why Jesus says we are "blessed" when we face oppression for serving his kingdom instead of the *default* "fallen" world's system.

And while we're discussing cataclysms, God doesn't send special storms of wrath and hate via disease, famine, or pestilence.[23] These have always occurred. And they will continue to happen. Natural disasters are just that: *natural.* Jesus expresses frustration with those who blame calamity on some special sin of the victims: "At that very time there were some present who told him about the Galileans whose blood Pilate had mingled with their sacrifices. He asked them, 'Do you think that because these Galileans suffered in this way they were worse sinners than all other Galileans? No, I tell you; but unless you repent, you will all perish as they did. Or those eighteen who were killed when the tower of Siloam fell on them—do you

20. Matthew 5:1–12.

21. Matthew 7:12.

22. See Isaiah 1:17; Isaiah 58:6–14; Micah 6:8; Matthew 11:2–6; and Matthew 25.

23. Many evangelical leaders have named certain storms and natural disasters as evidence of God's displeasure.

think that they were worse offenders than all the others living in Jerusa-lem? No, I tell you; but unless you repent, you will all perish just as they did."[24] Natural disasters are opportunities for humanity to show goodwill. We should see them as moments when we can reach out in solidarity with all people (friend and enemy) to be the kind of blessing Jesus has called us to be. *Not* to evangelize heavy-handedly, but to *bless* without expectation of anything in return, and to do so simply because those suffering are people made in the image of God and precious in God's sight.

Mainline theology suggests there will be only *one* return of Christ and only *one* judgment as presented in Matthew 25:

> When the Son of Man comes in his glory, and all the angels with him, then he will sit on the throne of his glory. All the nations will be gathered before him, and he will separate people one from another as a shepherd separates the sheep from the goats, and he will put the sheep at his right hand and the goats at the left. Then the king will say to those at his right hand, "Come, you that are blessed by my Father, inherit the kingdom prepared for you from the foundation of the world; for I was hungry and you gave me food, I was thirsty and you gave me something to drink, I was a stranger and you welcomed me, I was naked and you gave me clothing, I was sick and you took care of me, I was in prison and you visited me."[25]

The people who are placed on his right hand are baffled that they had min-istered to Jesus. That's because *literally* they didn't. They had served *others*. But Jesus credited their benevolence as though it had been done to him directly. The other group complains that they *would have served Jesus* if *he* had needed their aid. And Jesus berates them for *not* perceiving *him* in the poor and sick. Prior to this Jesus warns: "On that day many will say to me, 'Lord, Lord, did we not prophesy in your name, and cast out demons in your name, and do many deeds of power in your name?' Then I will declare to them, 'I never knew you; go away from me, you evildoers.'"[26] There is a human tendency to desire to perform flashy works instead of more mundane (and obscure) acts of kindness.[27] Jesus calls the Pharisees

---

24. Luke 13:1–5.

25. Matthew 25:31–36.

26. Matthew 7:22–23.

27. This self-aggrandizing theme is echoed in the story of the healing of Naaman in 2 Kings 5.

out for this penchant repeatedly. He clearly wants us to serve him in small and overlooked deeds—making a real difference one person at a time.[28]

When Jesus returns he is not going to judge people on arcane points of doctrine; he's going to ask if we helped others. And that's the point. Jesus wants us to see our foundational needs as met (spiritually and physically). After all, we are sons and daughters of God who are safe in the Father's hands. A "self-actualized" person is free to stop worrying about basic needs;[29] they are even free to do *without* them for a period of time. Such a person can stop worrying about himself or herself altogether, and strive to meet the needs of others! Followers of Christ need to be intentional about striving to build Christ's kingdom in the present by offering "cups of cold water" to those in need. We need to work diligently to bring justice and fairness to those who are marginalized around the world, and around us. We do this by standing against all those who exploit the poor and weak— even when that is our government, or our town's largest employer. This has been the focus of the vast majority of Christians throughout time. It is well within our grasp if we make it our priority as well.

28. See also Matthew 6, where he speaks of practicing alms and prayer in private.
29. Like food, clothing, shelter, and security.

6

Thy Kingdom Come

For Jesus, there are no countries to be conquered, no ideologies to be imposed, no people to be dominated. There are only children, women and men to be loved.

—HENRI NOUWEN[1]

The general who advances without coveting fame, and retreats without fearing disgrace, whose only thought is to protect his country and do good service for his sovereign, is the jewel of the kingdom.

—SUN TZU[2]

WHEN THE DISCIPLES ASKED Jesus to teach them to pray, he gave them "The Lord's Prayer."[3] It's far more than just a model prayer or a set of words to rattle off rote. This prayer teaches us several important truths. It's a sort of "Pledge of Allegiance" for the kingdom of God. It teaches us to speak several *realities* to God, and one another. All of them are vital to a healthy Christian perspective on life. The prayer begins: "Our Father in heaven." We share a brother/sisterhood with *all of humanity* because we share the same "Father."

1. As quoted by Dear, *Put Down Your Sword*, 138.

2. Sun Tzu, *On the Art of War*, 110.

3. This follows their question in Luke 11:2–4, but is offered without their asking in Matthew 6:9–13.

Some of our siblings may not recognize this,[4] but that changes nothing for *us*. We *do* know it.

God is the Father (Mother[5]) of all people, especially of those who believe in Jesus as the Messiah.[6] The prayer continues: "Hallowed is your name." "Hallowed" means *revered* or *greatly respected*. The very *idea* of God should call to mind everything that is best and most noble. And since God is our Father, it also ought to evoke in us behaviors that reflect him and should inspire us to live out those same values toward all of his creation.[7] Then we're told to say: "Thy kingdom come." And this is where "the rubber meets the road" for our purposes. We're taught to pray that God's kingdom come—that his *will* is done on Earth as it is in heaven. The point in praying this is summed up in Luther's *Small Catechism*: "God's kingdom comes on its own without our prayer, but we ask in this prayer that it may also come to us."[8]

Jesus established a *kingdom* when he was on Earth two thousand years ago. Many fundamentalists and evangelicals miss this, partly because we live in a "representative republic," under a democratic form of government and not in a proper kingdom. Americans feel, rightly or wrongly, that we are active participants in our own governance. We take the first three words of the Constitution, "We the people," seriously. We believe in a government that is: "of the people, by the people, and for the people.[9] And that's a nice mythology! It galvanized the United States as a nation with a common belief system and shared values. But all that came along eighteen hundred years after Jesus. No one, including him, thought in those terms in the first century. That era was marked by decidedly different political realities. For the vast majority of human history *kings formed their own kingdoms*. They

---

4. The largest evangelical church in my town placed the following quote on their front sign a couple years ago: "Most people who say 'Our Father' are really just orphans." Their pastor regularly preached that Catholics, Episcopalians, and Lutherans were "bound for hell."

5. There are several Bible passages that allude to God as Mother: Isaiah 66:13; Psalm 131:2; Matthew 23:37; Luke 13:34.

6. 1 Timothy 4:10.

7. "Sin" is a relational word, not a legal one. Sin is any thought, word, or deed that strays from the "bullseye" of perfectly reflecting God's character.

8. Luther, *Small Catechism*, 19.

9. Lincoln, "Gettysburg Address."

did it by *declaring* it so, and backing up their claim with bribes, threats, intimidation, and especially with armies.[10]

I mentioned in chapter 4 that when John the Baptizer, Jesus, or the apostles "preach," "proclaim," or "announce" the kingdom of God they are doing something specific. Those translations all reflect what the Greek word *kerussein* means . . . sort of. The problem is, we don't think of those words like a first-century person would. In fact, "preach" has become something far more common in English than the word originally meant. "Proclaim" or "announce" still retain some of their former dignity, but they have become eroded through excessive use as well. The main thought behind the Greek word *kerussein* isn't broadcasting a message as much as it is the *authority* behind the message. When John the Baptizer "preached," he did so *as a prophet of God*. His message was to be seen as *coming from God*. We read in Mark 1:2–3: "See, I am sending my messenger ahead of you, who will prepare your way; the voice of one crying out in the wilderness: 'Prepare the way of the Lord.'" The Gospel is quoting both Isaiah 40:3 and Malachi 3:1. It sees fulfillment of these Old Testament prophecies in John the Baptizer as *anointed by God* to convey *his message*. Because of that, John the Baptizer's words were "official." They communicated official kingdom business. The Gospels view John the Baptizer as a special *emissary* of God whose divine task was to prepare people to receive their king—Jesus. Later, Jesus appoints his Twelve to do the same thing *in his name*. The biblical word applied to them is "apostle." The word "apostle" means "to send out with a commission." So their words were not so much their *own opinion* as they were the intentions of the one who sent them: Jesus—and *ultimately* God.

This requires a certain amount of faith. And that's another place things have veered off track in the theological thinking of most modern American evangelicals and fundamentalists. They have come to believe that we need to place our *faith* in certain *doctrinal positions*—especially the theology of the "Sinners' Prayer." Over the years I've spoken with a surprising number of confused people who are afflicted with spiritual anxiety tied to this formidable guardian of salvation. Many people worry whether (or not) they have *stated* everything *necessary* to gain entry into heaven after they die—which is sadly what "salvation" has become in the minds of far too many American Christians. Many evangelicals will admit that they've felt it necessary to "accept Jesus into their hearts," not just once, but *several* times. They've been prompted to do this at the hands of sincere Christians who

---

10. Not a lot has changed. I'd recommend Noam Chomsky on this topic.

have no idea what a mess they're making of things. "Faith," to fundamentalists and evangelicals, boils down to believing the correct things *about* Jesus, and *articulating* those tenets to him in a prayer of *acceptance*. The "Sinners' Prayer" has become a *shibboleth* that must be spoken correctly in order to gain salvation. But biblical faith isn't a list of things we're supposed to believe *about* Jesus; faith is *trust in* Jesus as king of a countercultural kingdom.

Back to the confused saints I've spoken with: most of them have been told that they "accepted" Jesus *wrong* whenever they did it previously in their lives.[11] Usually, they've been told their acceptance was flawed because they *omitted* something vital in their original prayer. For instance, a young woman came to my office recently and told me she had accepted Jesus five times in her life. She was perplexed and uncertain if she had finally done it "right" a few weeks before. She was making the rounds to several churches and getting the opinions of several clergy, which is both commendable and tragic! She said the first time she was "saved" was when she was a preteen. In high school someone informed her she couldn't have *meant it* enough, because she was too young, so had her first *redo*. As a young college student, a preacher told her she wasn't really saved because she didn't *say* she believed in the virgin birth. When she protested she'd always believed that, he told her it didn't matter: if she didn't *say it* in her prayer she was still lost in her sins. So she had her second redo. At a revival service a few years later, an evangelist preached that anyone who had committed *certain sins*[12] had forfeited the grace of their salvation, and needed to be "resaved." She had committed one of the *arbitrary* offenses, so she did it again. Finally, just a few weeks before coming to see me, a local minster[13] told his flock (where she attended) that unless they had told Jesus that they believed in the *rapture*, they weren't really saved—he also added a "must do" list, which included *tithing*. That wasn't on the former guy's list of prohibitions, so she was *doubly damned* all over again!

My heart breaks for the *fear* these people live in. My blood boils that other clergy, well-meaning and sincere or not, inflict these types of doubts into the minds of people. They are inflicting great harm on children of God! What's tacitly implied whenever people teach this sort of thing is that God

11. I realize this is not proper English; it's done for emphasis.

12. The list was: affairs, abortions, homosexual acts, heterosexual anal sex, drug use, viewing pornography, and going to strip clubs. Apparently murder, theft, and lying aren't spiritually fatal, but flipping through *Playboy* is. Who gets to decide this stuff?

13. The one with the "Our Father" sign.

is a total jerk.[14] They essentially reduce God into a celestial lawyer who's doing everything he can to deny "payout" on a *salvation claim*. He's inspecting all the "fine print." And if every "t" isn't crossed, and every "i" dotted *just so*, he shakes he's head and consigns the offender to an eternity in conscious torment! "Unconditional love" indeed!

Such a God is an abomination to the Yahweh of Scripture! *Nowhere* in the Gospels does Jesus ask anyone to "invite him into their heart."[15] He never says anything about having to publically articulate "belief" in his mother's virginity at the time of his conception. He never speaks of tithing or the so-called rapture at all. His message is: "Repent, for the kingdom of heaven has come near."[16] The kingdom "has come near," especially because the king has come near. But "faith" is required to see it. That's because there's still: a Caesar in Rome, a King Herod in Jerusalem, and Pilate in the Antonia fortress, overshadowing the temple court. In other words, it doesn't *look* like Jesus is king at all. Nothing about him, from his birth in a stable to his crucifixion on Golgotha, looks noble or kingly. But *that's* his message—his claim—*nonetheless*. *That's* the claim that got him sideways with the priests and Pharisees. *That's* the claim that finally convinced Pilate to become mixed up with the internal politics of the Jews. *That's* the claim he makes to us.

In the earliest churches, formal creedal statements were not common. Those came along later to define particular "approved" doctrines of the evolving church. The greatest creeds of Christianity have a lot more to do with *politics* than theology—they came into play after the church became the *official religion* of Rome. Those creeds served to enforce *uniformity* for imperial benefit, not religious purposes. The shortest of these is the Apostles' Creed, which emerged in about 390 CE.[17] The earliest is the Nicene Creed of 325 CE.[18] And, finally the Athanasian Creed was approved in the

---

14. I want to say "raging asshole," but the last time I said that to someone they got the vapors.

15. This image likely comes from Revelation 3:20, where Jesus speaks to *Christians* at Laodicea.

16. Matthew 4:17.

17. But was altered up until the seventh century.

18. Though it too was altered in 381 CE.

sixth century.[19] There are several creedal snippets in the New Testament: the most common seems to have been simply: "Jesus is Lord."[20]

And this is where we're handicapped by *our* political expectations. In 27 BCE a man named Octavian was made Caesar and given the name/title "Augustus." He was proclaimed to be a "Son of God." He was also referred to as "Savior of the People." You may have read scholarship or seen documentaries that claim Jesus' titles were not unique to him, but were *copied* from predecessors and applied to Jesus secondarily. And that's *true*! Some people use that fact to dismiss Christianity as some sort of hack job on history. They claim early Christians borrowed several beliefs extant in the ancient world, cobbling them together to form a new religion. The major problem with such a theory is that these supposedly invented claims would have tricked no one in the first and second centuries. Early Christians knew full well these titles were claimed by the Caesars, and counter-claimed by Jesus. Everyone in the first- and second-century Roman Empire was expected to at least *pretend* to ascribe these titles solely to the various Caesars. Attributing them to Jesus was *illegal*, and was the cause of myriad *executions*! Many Christians refused to say, "Caesar is Lord," with *all* that implied. They believed the real "Lord/King," "Son of God," and "Savior of the People" was Jesus, not Caesar. And they were willing to die for *that* belief.

As we've discussed, Christ's "kingdom" is a *present reality*. It began while Jesus was on Earth and continues *now*.[21] The book of Revelation teaches *that reality* too. Revelation is written with seven "cycles," largely covering the same themes from different points of view. The first of these cycles covers the first three chapters: the introduction through the seven letters to the seven churches. John (the stated author) specifically says that Jesus is the "Ruler of the kings of the earth."[22] John also says Jesus has caused all his followers to be a "Kingdom, priests serving his God and Father."[23] This notion is woven all through the New Testament epistles as a present reality.

In Revelation 1:9 John the Divine says he shares an experience with us, a universal reality common to all Christians of all time and all places.

19. These are the ecumenical creeds of Western Christianity—not all Eastern churches acknowledge them.

20. Found in 1 Corinthians 12:3 and Romans 10:9; see also Philippians 2:11 and Romans 1:3–4.

21. Theologians refer to this approach to interpreting Revelation as "amillennialism."

22. Revelation 1:5.

23. Revelation 1:6; a theme also expressed in 1 Peter 2:9.

He says: "I, John, your brother share with you in Jesus the persecution, and the kingdom, and the patient endurance." Understanding *this* is critical to comprehending the rest of what is to be "revealed" in the "Apocalypse." The book of Revelation is all about *"revealing"* things that are hidden: *peeling back the false façade to display the true reality beneath the surface.* That's the mystery of Revelation. It's not about foretelling the future; it's about revealing the true reality of the present that lay *hidden* under a faux exterior. John's visions do that by flashing from the "reality" people on Earth *can see* around them, to the reality of "heaven."

The opening section (cycle) of the book of Revelation begins with a vision of Christ walking in the midst of seven lampstands, which represent seven churches. These congregations experience different levels of persecution and wrestle with different failings. But each experiences difficulties that are still common in churches today, such as: emphasizing "pure" theology at the expense of genuine, sacrificial love (Ephesus); being paralyzed by fear of getting into trouble with the government (Smyrna); and resting on the laurels of the past and "sleeping," doing nothing of value for the kingdom of Christ in the present[24] (Sardis). The message is universal. Jesus claims to be king of all.

The second cycle (Revelation 4:1–8:5) involves the literary motif of opening seals on a scroll. Again Christ is represented as king in heavenly glory: "In heaven stood a throne, with one seated on the throne! . . . And the four living creatures, each of them with six wings, are full of eyes all around and inside. Day and night without ceasing they sing, 'Holy, holy, holy, the Lord God the Almighty, who was and is and is to come.'"[25] Jesus is presented as the only person able to break the seals and reveal the genuine reality of world history that lay hidden behind the façade we see around us.[26] As each seal is broken an earthly devastation is revealed: things that our daily experience has dulled us to—like polluted air and water. However, each of these realities is foreign to God's original order. The breaking of the seal informs us anew how anomalous our reality is to that of God's intent.

Jesus enters our fallen existence as "the Lion of the tribe of Judah, the Root of David,"[27] and begins the long process of setting things right during

---

24. Jesus actually suggests that these people had soiled their pants in their spiritual slumber in Revelation 3:4.

25. Revelation 4:2, 8, a passage that calls to mind both Isaiah 6 and Ezekiel 1.

26. A similar apocalyptic motif is expressed in the *Matrix* trilogy.

27. Revelation 5:5.

his earthly ministry. He continues that work through *our* efforts today. It will be fully completed when he returns on the Last Day. He can undertake this task because he alone has "conquered" the *fruit* of the primordial fall of humanity—Death. Obviously, the introduction of a figure called "the Lion of the tribe of Judah, the Root of David" elicits a certain expectation—one of great military might and physical power (akin to King David). But that expectation of *majesty* is dashed when the "Lion" turns out to be a *"Lamb"* who has been *slaughtered*! This is the great mystery, which can only be *revealed* to us by God! It's exactly the opposite of what we're naturally inclined to think. Rapture theology misses this point. Modern rapture commentators, thinking from *within* our fallen paradigm, suggest that Jesus *causes* the worldwide devastation we see as he sequentially unfastens each of the seals depicted. That's totally out of character with everything we know of Jesus!

Most mainline theology teaches that as Jesus opens each seal he is *revealing* for our eyes what *fallen humanity has been doing* (and continues to do) throughout history. As the four horsemen gallop forth when their seals are opened, Jesus is *showing us* what *has been happening* since Cain slew Abel. The apocalyptic horsemen represent *all* violent and destructive human activity over the ages. The last three seals are a synopsis of satanic (supernatural) activity that has been working counter to God and his creation since the dawn of time.[28] In the center of this second vision cycle is this verse: "You [Jesus] are worthy to take the scroll and to open its seals, for you were slaughtered and by your blood you ransomed for God saints from every tribe and language and people and nation; you have made them to be a kingdom and priests serving our God, and they will reign on earth."[29] It is the same theme we saw in the first cycle. Jesus established God's kingdom

---

28. The white horse represents human empires: government-sanctioned violence toward anyone opposing the growth and expansion of the state; the red horse stands for human violence wrought of self-interest, whether it be gangs, mobs, or individual viciousness; the black horse symbolizes famine (*note* that *wheat and barley* (the main food of the poor) *are affected,* but *not wine or olive oil,* which are luxury items, the purview of the rich, who rarely suffer like the poor); and the pale horse is "Death," and Hades travels with him. This is the partnership between fallen mankind and satanic hatred of all of God's creation. The link between heaven and Earth is revealed with the fifth seal, where we see the martyrs who were killed for God's kingdom. The sixth seal depicts an *earthquake,* an apocalyptic trope used to portray God *shaking fallen humanity's work off of his good creation*—it depicts the "Last Day." With the seventh seal there is "silence in heaven." This is a dramatic device serving like a curtain dropping in a play, allowing the stage to be set for the next scene.

29. Revelation 5:9.

by his ministry, death, and resurrection. We have been initiated into *that* kingdom as priests—whose job it is to stand between God and fallen mankind offering his ministrations of grace and mercy, as Jesus did before us. We *are* representatives of the kingdom, laboring in his name to expand it.

From Revelation 8:6 through Revelation 11, the third cycle is expressed under the symbol of trumpets sounding. Again drawing from the book of Isaiah, we read: "On that day the Lord will thresh from the channel of the Euphrates to the Wadi of Egypt, and you will be gathered one by one, O people of Israel. And on that day a great trumpet will be blown, and those who were lost in the land of Assyria and those who were driven out to the land of Egypt will come and worship the Lord on the holy mountain at Jerusalem."[30] Trumpets are sounded for several reasons in the Bible: for battles, warnings, retreats, and for calling assemblies. But nowhere in the Scriptures are trumpets blown which only *select* people hear, which is how the "rapture" is initiated in dispensational premillennialism. This is another fatal flaw of the rapture theory! It is *ridiculous* exegesis.[31]

This cycle shows us that God allows fallen man to "trample" his outer courtyard (the physical world), but the spiritual, inner court of "heaven" is still in order. Christians are a part of that reality, even ones who are being persecuted in this life. God is calling through the seven trumpets for people to recognize the futility of *human thinking*. He sends his witnesses—including us—to point to the true reality revealed in the Apocalypse.

The kingdom conflict reaches new heights in the fourth cycle, chapters 12–14: the visions cycle. The first tableau depicts Mary, bringing Jesus forth, only to have him caught up to heaven immediately. The focus shifts to Mary as a trope for the church living in the "wilderness."[32] During this span of time the devil attempts to destroy her, but God preserves her. Satan's

---

30. Isaiah 27:12–13. For additional context see: Joel 2, Zephaniah 1, Zechariah 9, 1 Corinthians 15, 1 Thessalonians 4, and Matthew 24.

31. Trumpets are used in the Old Testament to summon God's people to the Promised Land and to the temple, where they will be free to worship and serve God. This section of Revelation has striking and undeniable parallels to the ten plagues visited on Egypt, a common symbol of the entirety of the fallen world. The trumpets call us to see God leading us *out of "Egypt" and into his emerging kingdom*, as his temple. The trumpet visions follow the same basic pattern as the seals: the first four reflect mankind's activity in harming creation, and the last three are supernatural in origin. They speak to the *whole span of time* from the "fall" in Eden through the present. Humanity has damaged vegetation, salt water, fresh water, and the air, according to the text. However, the amounts are a bit higher than in the previous cycle, indicating a progression over time.

32. Having been carried there on "eagles' wings"—see Exodus 19:4 and Isaiah 40:31.

surrogates, the Beast from sea (world governments), and the Beast from the land (false religions—often mimicking the Lamb!) fare no better. Angels fly through the heavens calling out God's good news. The first proclaims the kingdom reign of Christ, followed closely by a second who announces the futility of human governance. A third announces that those who trust in human endeavors for peace and stability will reap the same destruction humans have always produced.[33] All people are presented as bearing one of two "marks" on their heads and hands: either the "mark" of the world system,[34] or God's name is scrolled on them.[35]

The fifth cycle in Revelation 15–16—the censor or bowl cycle—offers little that is new. This cycle is marked by two words: "Babylon" and "*porno*." Babylon always depicts something bad in Scripture.[36] It packs a huge punch, scripturally. The other word, *porno*, is a common Greek word. It's best translated as "whore." That's a jarring word for polite Christians, and it's supposed to be. A whore, in Scripture, isn't quite the same thing as a prostitute or a sex slave. People enter into prostitution out of desperation, real or perceived. They see no other viable choices for *survival*. And sex slaves generally have no choices at all. That isn't the case with whores. A whore is someone who has no immediate *need* for food, clothing, or shelter. They "sell themselves" for the experience, power, perverse pleasure—for numerous reasons—but none of them include *survival*. A whore chooses whoredom for no *good* reason.[37]

Revelation 17 presents Christians, who are supposed to be the "Bride" of Christ, playing the *whore* with government. It's vital for us to understand God isn't referring to atheists, agnostics or Muslims here. He's referring to Christians—his "Bride." He wants us to sit up and take notice. He views those who claim to be his followers but chose to embrace the *ways of the world*[38] as *whores*. This is particularly true for Christians who wed worldly ambitions to *national pride* (represented by the first Beast). The "Whore

33. Revelation 14:6–9.

34. Revelation 13:18.

35. Revelation 14:1.

36. It is *possibly* the place implied by the town named Enoch in Genesis 4, the "walled city" Cain builds after he flees the presence of God following the murder of his brother. It is *certainly* associated with the site of a ziggurat built by Nimrod in Genesis 11. We know that structure as the "Tower of Babel." It is *definitely* indicative of the capitol city of Nebuchadnezzar, who destroyed Solomon's temple and dragged many Israelites into captivity.

37. See the whole book of Hosea, where the nation of Israel is compared to a whore.

38. Violence, neglect, exploitation, greed, slander, etc; instead of his Beatitudes.

of Babylon" isn't some demonic Middle Eastern dictator. It's any Christian who tries to love God and money.[39] At any given time, it could be me—or *you!*

Christians are expected to embrace a different kingdom—a different husband—one that lives *under* the visible kingdoms of the state. In fact, the New Testament routinely tells us to submit to, and pray for, our temporal leaders ... whether or not we like them, their policies, or their religion.[40] The Scriptures actually tell us: "Religion that is pure and undefiled before God, the Father, is this: to care for orphans and widows in their distress, and to keep oneself unstained by the world";[41] and: "Will you call this a fast, a day acceptable to the Lord? Is not this the fast that I choose: to loose the bonds of injustice, to undo the thongs of the yoke, to let the oppressed go free, and to break every yoke? Is it not to share your bread with the hungry, and bring the homeless poor into your house; when you see the naked, to cover them, and not to hide yourself from your own kin?"[42]

My hope is that you are beginning to realize that there's a rich church tradition that sees the kingdom of God differently from the modern American travesty popularly called "rapture theology." Those who follow dispensational premillennialism are not evil or ill meaning. But their interpretation of the Bible is conceived of *democratic* ideals and born of *American* values. It is anachronistic and egocentric. It's wrong—and it matters!

The Scriptures present God's kingdom as a reality that's already here. We're invited to begin partaking of it in the church. And we're urged to participate in furthering it in the world. For Jesus this typically means opposing the default system and values of the world. In Scripture "religion" is *more* about solving other people's problems than it is about getting ourselves out of eternal condemnation.[43] We are directed to do that using the ideals Jesus presents in the Beatitudes, and elsewhere. This kingdom will never fully be revealed until the king arrives.[44] But in the meantime we have work to do preparing the way for him. It involves untying those in bondage, feeding the hungry, and blessing our enemies in Christ's name, and for his sake.

39. Matthew 6:24.

40. 1 Timothy 2:1–3; Romans 13:1; 1 Peter 2:17, etc.

41. James 1:27.

42. Isaiah 58:5b–7.

43. See Romans 12:1 and James 1:27.

44. See Isaiah 58, Matthew 25, and Revelation 21–22.

7

It's a Nice Day for a White Wedding[1]

my blood approves,
and kisses are better fate
than wisdom

—E.E. COMMINGS[2]

Madness is something rare in individuals—
but in groups, parties, peoples, and ages, it is the rule.

—FRIEDRICH NIETZSCHE[3]

IN THE CHURCH TODAY there are few debates that are more impassioned than what constitutes a God pleasing marriage.[4] Most evangelicals and fundamentalists were outraged by the 2015 U.S. Supreme Court ruling in

1. Idol, *White Wedding*.
2. e.e. commings. "since feeling is first," 93.
3. Nietzsche, *Beyond Good and Evil.*, 98.
4. Roman Catholics consider marriage a "sacrament." For them that means it must be performed by a priest. Protestants don't consider marriage a sacred rite, but many still think it's something best performed by an ordained minister. They usually accept a wedding presided over by a judge, JP, or ship captain as valid, but most Christians seem to believe that it's best for a couple, especially a Christian couple, to be married by a member of the clergy in a church. Scripturally, that's actually an odd expectation.

Obergefell v. Hodges—aka the "same-sex decision." Our evangelical and fundamentalist friends insist the Bible *clearly* teaches God intends for marriage to be between *one man* and *one woman*. They typically point to Adam and Eve as "proof" of this convention. And that's one more reason a *literal interpretation* of that mythic story is so critical to them—it reinforces several societal mores that are comfortable *for them*. But I suggest many of these so-called norms lack any actual moral *imperative* from the Bible. While most evangelicals and fundamentalists refer to *their view* as "biblical marriage," that simply doesn't work for several reasons. Most notably, there's a total lack of biblical command.

There are scores exceptions to the "one man/one woman" rule in the Bible. First there are numerous prominent (and "blessed") men who break this supposed rule: Abraham had a wife, *and* a servant girl, Hagar, as a sexual surrogate; Jacob married *two* sisters and fathered children by both of them, *and* by both of their handmaidens;[5] David had multiple wives and numerous concubines (sex slaves); and prolific Solomon had a total of one thousand women in his bed. Second, further complicating matters, there are actual rules found in the pages of the Bible that run counter to the spurious "biblical marriage" decree: Old Testament law requires a man who rapes a virgin to marry her—she has no choice in the matter (though the rapist is required to pay a "fine" to her *dad*);[6] and the Old Testament also obliges brothers-in-law of any Israelite widow without a son to be inseminated by them until she bears one, so the dead brother's lineage isn't lost.[7]

Let me be quick to affirm my belief that monogamy is right and proper. But I didn't form that conclusion along the same lines evangelicals and fundamentalists formed theirs. The New Testament does require monogamy, for

5. The fruit of those unions became the twelve Old Testament patriarchs. One of the passages outlining this is Genesis 30:1–8: "When Rachel saw that she bore Jacob no children, she envied her sister; and she said to Jacob, 'Give me children, or I shall die!' Jacob became very angry with Rachel and said, 'Am I in the place of God, who has withheld from you the fruit of the womb?' Then she said, 'Here is my maid Bilhah; go in to her, that she may bear upon my knees and that I too may have children through her.' So she gave him her maid Bilhah as a wife; and Jacob went in to her. And Bilhah conceived and bore Jacob a son. Then Rachel said, 'God has judged me, and has also heard my voice and given me a son'; therefore she named him Dan. Rachel's maid Bilhah conceived again and bore Jacob a second son. Then Rachel said, 'With mighty wrestlings I have wrestled with my sister, and have prevailed'; so she named him Naphtali." This passage became central to the theology embraced by the leaders of Margaret Atwood's *The Handmaid's Tale*.

6. Deuteronomy 22:28–29.

7. Deuteronomy 25:5–6.

pastors and deacons, anyway.[8] But the Bible *never* requires it for all men and women, and it's a giant leap into *dishonesty* to say it does. Reason and Scripture have had a large role in the formation of my views on this matter. One might say the Spirit has guided me (and a host of others) to see *past* the literal letter of scriptural law and example. My conclusion is based on the *trajectory* that I find in the pages of the Bible. Christians who claim the Bible reflects a *single expression* for marriage either don't know the facts or choose to ignore them because they're inconvenient. The notion of "biblical marriage" is a fable invented by evangelicals and fundamentalists. And they aren't currently pushing it to reinforce heterosexual monogamy nearly as much as they are to fend off gay marriage. They want to lend moral credibility and scriptural authority to their bigotry. But the equality of committed homosexual monogamy (marriage) to heterosexual marriage is actually two separate issues for American Christians. One is secular and the other is religious.

Obergefell v. Hodges only addresses its *legality* under the Constitution, the *secular* concern. The Supreme Count found that it *is* legal for homosexuals to enter into marriages in the United States based on both the Due Process Clause and the Equal Protections Clause of the Fourteenth Amendment to the Constitution. Whenever evangelicals and fundamentalists wish to set aside established law in favor of their religious beliefs, they are revealing their impulse to suppress others' freedoms because of their interpretation of divine will.[10]

The second issue is a *religious* one: it concerns what God says on the matter. Evangelicals and fundamentalists blend the two together because they have created another folktale: the legend that America is a "Christian nation." But the Supreme Court, or any court, has no more business basing its decisions on the Bible than they do basing them on the Koran or the Egyptian Book of the Dead. The First Amendment clearly states that no religion (or religious book) will be given any official or established status above (or below) any other.

But as Christians we must consider what God wants *us* to do! So let's ponder marriage—gay, straight, monogamous, and/or polyamorous—biblically

8. 1 Timothy 3:2.

9. And to bolster "complementarianism"—or scripturally sanctioned sexism.

10. It's a hallmark of church. Can you imagine if Muslims did this? Or Satanists? Holy hysteria!

11. As we discussed in detail in chapter 4, America is not a Christian nation, it is a secular nation, and only the second part of the question concerns us as Christians and as congregations.

and theologically. Who performed weddings in the Old Testament? What do they look like in the Bible? Genial couples never went to the temple or synagogue to be joined together as husband and wife by a priest of the Aaronic lineage. They never required the presence of a recognized and credentialed rabbi. Biblical marriages (in the actual Bible) look a lot more like this: A man who had a source of income would save up a bit of money and approach another man who had a young daughter of about fourteen to sixteen; they would work out a price—egads! The couple would be "betrothed," which means they were all but married; the only thing lacking was the "knowing" part.[12] The groom had up to a year to come claim his wife, who would continue to live with her dad until he arrived to take physical possession of her.[13] It's not very romantic to consider being sold to the highest bidder, but that's more nearly how it worked. The Bible neither praises nor condemns this, it simply *reports* it. A priest was never involved.[14] A marriage was essentially a *business deal* struck between the father of a girl and a man who needed a mate—or a *replacement mate*.[15] So the man buying you from your dad might be a lot older than you. In fact, he might be your dad's best friend, or a guy your father owed a lot of money . . . he might even be your uncle, or cousin. And we mustn't lose sight of the fact that the "dad" in this scenario was often a step-dad, a man who married your mother after your bio-dad died. He may, or may not, have any concern about your "happiness." The groom-to-be might be after a second, third, or subsequent mate—not to replace one who's died, but to compliment his growing harem.[16]

There's still no priest involved, nor was the temple or synagogue. But the local pub probably was! That's because, while there was no "church service," there was a *party*—which often went on for days. And that means food and drink. Remember Jesus' first miracle in the Gospel of John? He made around 160 gallons of wine. There are about twenty-one six-ounce glasses of wine in a gallon. Meaning, Jesus made about 3,360 glasses of wine, for a feast that had already been going on for a while!

---

12. I mean that in the *biblical sense*.

13. All those Gospel stories where Jesus says something about a groom coming at night to claim his wife, and her not knowing when, are built on this common practice.

14. Unless the dad or the groom happened to be a priest.

15. The mortality rate among childbearing women was fairly high.

16. This was more rare in Jesus' day than in more remote times, but it still occurred.

As we move into the New Testament, we have to ask how many weddings are presented to us, and the answer is very few. And none of them appear to be significantly different from the Old Testament ones. Jesus never presides at one—except as a substitute *bartender*. Neither do Peter, James, John or any of the later church leaders like Paul, Timothy, or Onesimus. And while we're at it, when did the couple sign the marriage license? And to whom did they mail it? Right! There wasn't one. A marriage was generally a business arrangement between a father and another man in which the father "sold" his daughter to a guy for some sheep, a cow, and a couple silver coins. They threw a big party and invited family and friends to come by and get sloshed in celebration. Religious figures weren't involved, nor was the synagogue or church. That's true "biblical marriage"!

The state wasn't really involved either, unless things went wrong and the husband sought a divorce (something that happened far more than most modern Americans realize).[17] In such cases the elders of the city made sure he gave the woman her dowry back, and perhaps a bit more to sustain her for a short while . . . until she found another husband to provide for her. That brings us to the real reason for the state's involvement in marriages: *inheritance*. It's all *business* for the state, too. They don't have a pressing concern about who sleeps with whom. But they do have to become involved (via courts) with *who* has a right to *what* after the man dies.

Marriage, as we practice it today, is mostly a *social construct*, not a reflection of biblical practices or requirements. We have become so accustomed to the *way things have been done* that we believe they have come to us *from* the Bible. But they have actually come from *culture*. The church got into the marriage business after the fall of Rome, when clergy started working for both the church and state.[18] Subsequently, the arrangement became "the way things were." But this arrangement is nowhere to be found in the Bible or in the early church. It is wholly without scriptural foundation or rationale.

And that brings us to "complementarianism." This is a theory that is alarmingly popular in evangelical and fundamentalist churches today. While it

---

17. I'm not going to get into all this again here, but there were three factions of rabbis in Jesus day, one of which was generally opposed to divorce (Shammai), while the other two schools (Hillel and especially Akiba) were more tolerant. This explains why Jesus was asked to weigh in on the divorce question—to determine which school he was friendlier with. See chapter 4 for more information.

18. They were only people capable of doing many jobs, after all the rest of *literate* society fled to Constantinople.

reflects *attitudes* that were fairly common prior to the 1950s in both church and secular society, the contemporary manifestation is found almost exclusively within very conservative Christian, Jewish, or Islamic enclaves. The Christian expression of this theory points to the Genesis account as a literal expression of male and female *differentness*. Proponents believe this differentness is rooted in a literal creation of only two humans: a man named Adam and a woman named Eve. Eve, they contend, was made to complete and serve Adam. The view essentially *ignores* Genesis 1:26–28, 30b–31:

> Then God said, "Let us make humankind in our image, according to our likeness; and let them have dominion over the fish of the sea, and over the birds of the air, and over the cattle, and over all the wild animals of the earth, and over every creeping thing that creeps upon the earth." So God created humankind in his image, in the image of God he created them; male and female he created them. . . . And it was so. God saw everything that he had made, and indeed, it was very good. And there was evening and there was morning, the sixth day.

Complementarianism derives its basis from the Genesis 2 account of creation, where egalitarianism is *suppressed* and a specific order is presented:

> The Lord God formed man from the dust of the ground, and breathed into his nostrils the breath of life; and the man became a living being. And the Lord God planted a garden in Eden, in the east; and there he put the man whom he had formed. . . . Then the Lord God said, "It is not good that the man should be alone; I will make him a helper as his partner." . . . So the Lord God caused a deep sleep to fall upon the man, and he slept; then he took one of his ribs and closed up its place with flesh. And the rib that the Lord God had taken from the man he made into a woman and brought her to the man. Then the man said, "This at last is bone of my bones and flesh of my flesh; this one shall be called Woman, for out of Man this one was taken." Therefore a man leaves his father and his mother and clings to his wife, and they become one flesh.[19]

Complementarians find in the latter passage a *command*. Specifically, they believe this passage *requires* men to be "in charge" of women, especially their wives and daughters. They use this passage to suppress women and to require female submission to men as a *divine* warrant, a part of the "literal" creation blueprint. They teach that this command is still in force. Leadership,

---

19. Genesis 2:7–8, 18, 20–24.

according to complementarians, is always supposed to be in the hands of men, and it is God's will that women embrace the role of supporting their men in every way, ideally without bickering and nagging. Many go further and insist Genesis 2 precludes the possibility of women serving as pastors, elders, presidents, or deacons within the church. Sometimes it is even used to disenfranchise women of the right to vote in congregational meetings.[20]

There are few New Testament passages that address marital dynamics, but we do have this: "Be subject to one another out of reverence for Christ. Wives, *x* to your husbands as you are to the Lord. For the husband is the head of the wife just as Christ is the head of the church, the body of which he is the Savior. Just as the church is subject to Christ, so also wives ought to be, in everything, to their husbands. Husbands, love your wives, just as Christ loved the church and gave himself up for her."[21] I made an adjustment in the text above to better reflect what the Greek *actually* says. I removed the words "be subject to"[22] following "Wives" and marked it with an *x*. I did that because it's *not* there in Greek. It's not a mistake to supply it in English because it is *implied*, but it's important that it's not in the original text. The only time the actual word "submit" or "be subject" occurs is in the beginning portion of this passage, and directly refers to *both* the husband and the wife offering submission to *each other*.

It begs notice, especially if you stop to think about the reality of the first century! There is no parallel Old Testament passage telling women to submit to their husbands—there was absolutely no need for that. It was an established reality. Any uppity woman could be *stoned*. Or, if you were a more "righteous" man, you could just divorce your headstrong wife and be rid of her that way. Of course, women were not afforded the same right to divorce their husbands if things weren't working out for them. Men had all the power; women were effectively second-class citizens.[23]

So what was going on in the first-century church that prompted Paul to feel the need to issue a generic kibosh to women? One might think they somehow got the idea they were the equals of their men. Perhaps they began acting like men routinely behaved. Maybe the predominantly Greek

---

20. Obviously this theory totally ignores Galatians 3:27–29.

21. Ephesians. 5:21–26.

22. Or "submit."

23. The Gospel of Mark 10:1–12 places the possibility of the *wife* initiating a divorce against her husband into the mouth of Jesus, which is fascinating because women could do no such thing in first-century Israel.

women who were in these congregations had begun following Jesus long before their men (like Lydia), and perchance they were subjugating men, the same way woman had been subjugated for millennia.[24] Could it be that these women were swinging the pendulum too far in the opposite direction?

The other notion in this passage is "headship." The husband is said to be the "head" of the wife—and Paul makes it clear what that involves: sacrificial love. The man is to lead the way in sacrifice, which in turn sets the tone for the woman reciprocating. This is novel, because it isn't rooted in some *ontological right* of the man as *superior* to the woman. It's based in service to the woman. It's not a command authority that Paul is speaking of; it is a *service* authority. And *this* is what's really *new* in his words, within a first-century context.[25] In Matthew 20:24–28 Jesus appeals to exactly the same kind of service authority when he tells his disciples how to lead his nascent church after his departure.

Under the teaching of the church, reflecting the obvious attitude of Jesus, women were beginning to believe that they were the equals of men, made in the same image of God. It seems quite clear from mosaics and other artistic depictions that women were serving as pastors in various places in the first several centuries of the church. Egalitarian views were taking hold quickly. In fact, so much so that it was becoming its own problem in some places. Women were beginning to *suppress* men. Apparently Paul felt this would have had disastrous consequences for the church if left unchecked. Paul seeks to correct it before it got out of hand.[26]

Biblically, men and women are completely equal in every regard. Husbands and wives in our twenty-first-century context should treat one another as fully equal partners in their marriage, and in life. Additionally, all offices of the church are available to both sexes. Paul writes the seminal passage of egalitarianism in his letter to the Galatians: "As many of you as were baptized into Christ have clothed yourselves with Christ. There is no longer Jew or Greek, there is no longer slave or free, there is no longer male and female; for all of you are one in Christ Jesus. And if you belong to

24. There *were* powerful priestesses in Greek lands, unlike Israel, so such an idea is far from inconceivable.

25. Paul was keenly aware that men thought they were better than women. It was commonly believed in the first century (and well beyond) that all "male seed" was *male*. The birth of a girl meant something had gone wrong. This was always perceived to be the woman's *fault*. Women and girls were popularly thought to be "defective males"!

26. Another main passage cited for support of complementarianism is 1 Timothy 2. It fits in under this same conversation, and adds little new which needs to be dealt with.

Christ, then you are Abraham's offspring, heirs according to the promise."[27] All who have been born into the kingdom of God, the church, through the waters of baptism have been fully covered in Christ and are *equal* in him. In case anyone isn't sure what the implications of this are, he says *all* human distinctions have been erased. Poor Gentile women are equal in every way to rich Jewish men in the church. That about covers that.

Today many churches are wrestling with a slightly different issue: couples who live together before they're *officially* married. There are several different approaches congregations and pastors take to this practice: some churches condemn it publically, but ignore it in practice; others require cohabitating couples to separate before they'll marry them; a few rush to marry them privately and perform a public celebration later; yet others ignore the issue in the interest of sparing feelings, but secretly fret about the "sinfulness" of the situation; and there are those (like me) who consider a cohabitating couple to be fully married in God's eyes, already, if not in the *state's* opinion.[28]

As we've seen, marriage was never the province of the temple, synagogue, or church. "Biblical marriage," if there is such a thing, is the purview of the *couple*. No longer does a father "sell" his daughter to another man, at least in modern America. A woman enters into this "contract" of her own free will. She speaks for herself, as does the groom. They "bind themselves together" as husband and wife. And couples that commit to living together in the fashion of husband and wife have done that—whether they have intended to or not. Consider Paul's words to the congregation at Corinth: "'All things are lawful for me,' but not all things are beneficial. . . . Do you not know that your bodies are members of Christ? Should I therefore take the members of Christ and make them members of a prostitute? Never! Do you not know that whoever is united to a prostitute becomes one body with her? For it is said, 'The two shall be one flesh.' But anyone united to the Lord becomes one spirit with him."[29] Obviously the context is different— these Christians were involving themselves in all kinds of perverse sexual practices (among other things), and claiming that *everything* was OK for Christians because Christ had "fulfilled" the law for them. They had gotten

27. Galatians 3:27–29.

28. Which is not a moral or religious problem, though it can become a huge problem *legally*. But that's a different matter, and not to be confused with divine morality.

29. 1 Corinthians 6:12, 15–18.

their heads wrapped around grace very well! *Too well*, if that's possible! As a result they were doing everything they wanted, without any concern for God or others. Dietrich Bonheoffer refers to this as "cheap grace."[30]

For our purposes, this passage addresses the act of sex as creating a marital bond. As Paul sees it, couples who have sexual relations create a *marriage* in God's eyes. In that sense, Paul is suggesting, there is no such thing as "premarital sex." Sex creates a marriage: no license is required, no preacher, no vows, no nothing! Therefore, if a person goes to a pagan temple or brothel and hires a partner for intercourse, they are *married*. Of course that was not what these misguided brothers and sisters were intending. They also had failed to consider how they were participating in the *human exploitation* that always implicitly accompanies sex trafficking. That is another vitally important topic, but outside our scope. Obviously, when a couple sets up house and cohabitates, they have joined themselves together. And that's not sinful or wrong. But scripturally it does imply a lifelong commitment. The bond is one that is intended to make both stronger than they were individually. Marriage calls us to think of ourselves as a team rather than as individual free agents; it requires us to make sacrifices of ourselves in order to bless the union. That is the same mystery that lay at the heart of being church. But, to return to our focus, the *power* to make this bond does not reside outside the couple. It exists *within* the two people making the commitment.

I would be both remiss and *cowardly* if I stopped here. *Obergefell v. Hodges* made marriage a legal possibility in all fifty states for same-sex couples. This has caused genuine angst in the minds of some Christians, especially in fundamentalist and evangelical circles. We need to spend a little time examining the Bible concerning this issue.[31]

Obviously you can't find this scenario in the Bible. There are many reasons for that, not the least of which includes the fact that societal peers (equals) engaging in same-sex relations would have been executed in most ancient societies. But that's not to suggest that same-sex relations was frowned upon in most of those same societies. It's only to say that sex between *equals* was. And that's not the same thing. It was perfectly normal in most ancient cultures for a wealthy man to exploit his male servants and

---

30. Bonheoffer, *Cost of Discipleship*, 45.
31. See Vines, *God and the Gay Christian*.

slaves. It was *expected* that soldiers would rape male captives.[32] It was often lauded for older men to have younger male lovers. Plato suggests this was the purest and best love.[33] Of course, men had to have sex with women too, whether they liked it much or not, because *that's* the only way to make more humans, which was seen as an absolute *duty* in most ancient societies.

The ancient world was a man's world. Women weren't considered equal to men, and therefore their companionship was second rate (in the minds of many men, anyway). Sex with women was second best, if you could do "better," as well. Of course, most men didn't have servants and slaves, so sex with other men was out of reach for them. They were limited to sex with women only; unless they visited a pagan temple where male prostitutes—men and boys—were available for hire. Paul addresses this topic several times in his letters to such places as Corinth where there were dozens of these places.

No one in the ancient world thought of themselves as "homosexual." People didn't consider themselves "heterosexual" either. Those binary absolutes are a more modern notion. The very word "homosexual," while *rooted* in Greek, is *not* an ancient word at all. It didn't exist in Bible times, or even at the time of the Reformation. It likely first appeared in print in 1869. While same-sex practices are ancient, there was no word for a person who was *exclusively* attracted to people of their same sex until after the American Civil War.[34] Many ancient people would engage in sex where they could get it, but there was an order of preference. And many wealthy men preferred sex with other men to sex with women because they considered men (even those of inferior social status) to be their ontological equal, and therefore superior to women. Their ability to procure male partners also set them apart from other men, because in their societal context it marked them as superior to most other men. They were the true "alpha males" of the world. Paul speaks into *this* context. That's vital to understanding what he means.

Many Christians have projected *their* personal aversion toward same-sexuality onto God and condemn it in *his* name. When Christians who claim *God* hates homosexuality are asked to *substantiate* their position from

---

32. Most experts in germane fields wouldn't regard this as sex, labeling it violence used to establish dominance.

33. Plato, "Symposium," 63.

34. It didn't have anything to do with the Civil War; I'm just trying to establish some chronological context.

the Scriptures they go to the same six[35] passages: Genesis 18–19 (Sodom and Gomorrah); Leviticus 20:13; some *might* point to Judges 19; Romans 1:24–32; 1 Corinthians 6:17–20; and 1 Timothy 1:8–11. So let's consider each of them.

You're probably already familiar with the myth of Sodom and Gomorrah. In the story, a couple angels go to Sodom to urge Lot to leave, because the city is guilty of "very grave sin." So (cutting to the chase) these angels, who appeared as regular men, go to Lot's house. The men of Sodom come along and beat on the door demanding Lot send them out so they could gang rape them—or as the English politely renders it: "Bring them out to us, so that we may know them."[36] Hospitality laws being what they were, Lot feels obliged to send his two virgin daughters out to them instead. The angels strike everyone with blindness, and in the end Lot leaves. His wife famously looks back and turns to salt. Righteous Lot ends up sleeping with his two daughters years later and sires children by them . . . but I digress.

The controversy surrounds *what* the terrible *sin* of Sodom *actually was* in the first place. Many assume it is homosexuality. They come to that conclusion because of the terrible scene where the men are seeking the two angelic visitors for sex. But that's about as "homosexual" as a gang rape at frat house is "heterosexual." Both are examples of *violence* and *exploitation.* Rape is not *consensual* sex. Most psychologists insist it isn't even sexual at all. It's something else entirely! But that's beside the point. The simple fact that same-sex rape was attempted in this story isn't proof that homosexual relations were the reason God had targeted the city for destruction. In fact, it's *not!* The Bible later provides a clear explanation of why the destruction took place: "This was the guilt of your sister Sodom: she and her daughters had pride, excess of food, and prosperous ease, but did not aid the poor and needy. They were haughty, and did abominable things before me; therefore I removed them when I saw it."[37] The Bible itself tells us exactly what Sodom did that was so terrible they merited being nuked by God—and it's got *nothing* to do with being gay. It was greed and complacency toward the marginalized in society. America needs to take note of that biblical fact![38]

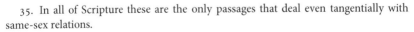

35. In all of Scripture these are the only passages that deal even tangentially with same-sex relations.

36. Genesis 19:5.

37. Ezekiel 16:49–50.

38. And while we're at it, the terrible myth of Sodom and Gomorrah really isn't as much about the destruction of the city due to God's wrath as it is about his *mercy.* In Genesis 18 God tells Abraham about his plan to destroy the wicked environs. And

In Leviticus 20:13 we read: "If a man lies with a male as with a woman, both of them have committed an abomination; they shall be put to death; their blood is upon them." The extended passage includes over a dozen prohibitions concerning sex. These include having sex with your sister, step-mom, aunt, daughter-in-law, mother-in-law, or your neighbor's wife. The passage also strictly forbids sex with your wife during her menstrual cycle, and sex with farm animals. It further says anyone who speaks complainingly about his parents should be put to death. And it restates the importance of not eating unclean animals like shrimp, catfish, rabbit, clams, lobster, crab, oysters, and pork. That means *bacon* was out, and bacon-wrapped shrimp was all kinds of delicious abomination! I bring this up simply to point out the obvious: anyone who cites this passage as "proof" also has to deal with *everything else* in it. Not many people are going fight for the right to have sex with their mother-in-law or farm animals, but I have never met anyone who believes that executing people for complaining about their parents is God-pleasing! And *bacon*, please! Most evangelicals and fundamentalists I know eat pork, and most are pretty fond of shellfish too. But those things are presented as forbidden in no uncertain terms in this *same passage*. I'm also just going to point out that exhaustive study of the phrase "lies with a male as with a woman" is a bit more ambiguous in Hebrew than it appears in English.[39] But it doesn't matter because the passage is already *fatally compromised* by the fact that it includes several other things none of us feel compelled to adhere to. Bacon.

In Judges 19 a story similar in many respects to Genesis 19 occurs in Gibeah, a city in the land of Benjamin. The men of this city seek to rape a Levite and he ends up sending his concubine (sex slave) out to them

Abraham bargains with God; he doesn't dispute the underlying problem or the justness of God's plan. But he does suggest that the presence of a very few righteous people should be sufficient to mitigate God's fury and preserve the cities. He says: "Far be it from you to do such a thing, to slay the righteous with the wicked, so that the righteous fare as the wicked! Far be that from you! Shall not the Judge of all the earth do what is just?" He begins his holy *bargaining* with fifty, and eventually "talks God down" to ten. God ultimately agrees to spare these *cities* if ten righteous people could be found within them. When even that low number could not be found, the angels *evacuated* the handful of "righteous" people they could find. Far from being a story about God wiping cities or countries off the map if they become a *little* wicked, this story shows us that the presence of 0.001 percent (ten people in an estimated ten thousand is a conservative guess of the population of the region) of compassionate and fair-minded people is adequate for God to "stay his hand."

39. This is sometimes a euphemism for male on male rape, as was especially common in ancient military contexts.

instead. They rape her to death. He takes her dead body home and chops her up into twelve pieces and mails her parts to the various tribes of Israel. (You can't make this stuff up!) The outrage galvanizes the other tribes against Gibeah—but the other Benjaminites[40] stand in solidarity with their morally bankrupt clansmen. In the end the tribe was eradicated except for a few men. So the rest of the Israelites feel bad for their cousins. They give them four hundred virgin girls from the other eleven tribes of Israel and urge them to *capture* women from Shiloh to breed the tribe back to life. This story isn't about being gay either; it's another tale of violence and exploitation.

In the New Testament the main passage cited in opposition to homosexuality is Romans 1:24–32. This passage speaks of same-sex relations—though the word "homosexuality" is never used. Verses 26–27 read: "For this reason God gave them up to degrading passions. Their women exchanged natural intercourse for unnatural, and in the same way also the men, giving up natural intercourse with women, were consumed with passion for one another. Men committed shameless acts with men and received in their own persons the due penalty for their error." The full passage lists about *two dozen* other offenses the people in question are *regularly guilty* of—including malice, greed, ruthlessness, murder, and inventing evil. Paul also says they are all God-haters. So the question is, is Paul talking about committed monogamous homosexuality, or something else? Perhaps something just as self-centered and exploitative as Sodom or Gibeah?

This is the biggest problem with assigning *certainty* to this passage; doing so essentially says that all homosexuals are guilty of the whole kit-and-caboodle outlined in Romans 1. Yet anyone who knows a few gay couples is forced to wince at the implication that they are evil and narcissistic in the way described in this passage. In fact most gay couples are anything but! They are regular people just like you and me.

Books abound discussing this passage, so I'm not going to spend any more time discussing it here. Suffice it to say a vast number of clergy and theologians are convinced Paul *doesn't* have committed, monogamous sexuality in mind. And our ranks are growing daily. If you read on to Romans 2, you'll see that Paul actually condemns *all* those who *judge*[41] others!

40. The tribe Gibeah was a part of.

41. "Judging" in the Scriptures generally means "to condemn" someone as "going to hell." It implies determining someone is so out of step with God that they are bound for an eternity of separation from God.

Some commentators speculate that in Romans 1 Paul is actually *repeating* a popular bias floating around in the Roman congregation, only to refute the whole flawed argument in Romans 2. One thing is certain: many of those who are busiest correcting what they believe to be a grievous sin in the lives of *others* are in fact heinously sinning *themselves!* Jesus says something similar: "Do not judge, so that you may not be judged. For with the judgment you make you will be judged, and the measure you give will be the measure you get. Why do you see the speck in your neighbor's eye, but do not notice the log in your own eye? Or how can you say to your neighbor, 'Let me take the speck out of your eye,' while the log is in your own eye? You hypocrite, first take the log out of your own eye, and then you will see clearly to take the speck out of your neighbor's eye."[42] *Aversion to judging needs to become a staple of the church!*

The only other spots in the New Testament that seem to address homosexuality are 1 Corinthians 6:9–10 and 1 Timothy 1:8–11. In these passages there are two words that are at the heart of the conversation. *Malakoi* is the English transliteration of one of those words, and it is rendered as "effeminate" in the King James Version (KJV) or "male prostitutes" in the New Revised Standard Version (NRSV); the *same word* is translated as "soft" in Matthew 11:8, where it is used in reference to priestly robes. The other is *arsenokoitai*, which is translated "sodomites" in the NRSV.[43]

The problem with these words is they were used differently in a first-century context.[44] Someone who was "soft" was seen as *womanly.* But that's only the beginning of understanding the term as it was used then. In Jesus' day women were thought to be defective men. They were understood to be wholly lacking in *control* of their passions, desires, and emotions. It was (manly) men who were in control of themselves. Men weren't perceived to be sex crazed and undisciplined *like women were.*[45] Men who were "soft," in the Roman Empire, were not, in fact, homosexuals, they were generally "straight"[46] guys who paid *excessive attention* to their looks, grooming, and clothing so they could seduce *ladies.* They were popularly considered to be as undisciplined as women.[47] Quite the opposite from being a term denot-

---

42. Matthew 7:1–5.

43. Published in 1989.

44. The word "homosexual" didn't even exist until 1800 years later.

45. See Plato's *Symposium* for a more full treatment of this.

46. Another term which is of modern origin, and used here simply for clarification.

47. Note: one of the seven virtues of the Roman *mos maiorum* ("way of the elders")

ing homosexuality, *malakoi* ("soft") is a term that would evoke the word "playboy" today. Sir Roger Moore's "James Bond" would be a great example of what the Romans would consider *malakoi*.

The other word, *arsenokoitai*, is a bit trickier. It's been suggested that Paul made this word up. When I was learning Greek I was taught that it only appears twice in *all* of literature—here in these two passages. But now, three decades later, we have found more occurrences of it. And that's changing a lot of things. Typically when the word is found in other ancient documents, it clearly refers to something other than "sodomy" or homosexual sex. It refers to the *exploitation* of someone—typically in a sexual manner. Pederasty,[48] especially for hire, is probably a better understanding of what Paul is aiming at: people who enslave children and pimp them out for pay—a practice that was tragically common in the first century.

I don't believe Paul could even envision openly gay committed couples (male or female). It simply wasn't part of his world. He was thinking of something totally different—lascivious, self-centered heterosexuality in the one case, and violent and exploitative homosexual prostitution of peri-adolescents (both boys and girls) in the other. And whatever was going on in Rome, it involves so many other things that homosexuality[49] was only one of nearly two dozen things he was concerned with—things that simply do not pertain to most gay people and/or couples today, rendering the passage *ambiguous* at best.

The Bible does not condemn homosexual people or practice within a monogamous and egalitarian context. Homosexuals are not "going to hell." God, however, does want homosexuals to express their sexuality within the bounds of committed relationships (just like "straight" people). God wants his followers oppose violence, exploitation, and judging people who are different from us. May the church keep this fact foremost in her mind as she deals with others!

was *virtus*, which is derived from *vir*, meaning the "ideal man." This ideal of Roman culture stressed that *real* men knew what was good and evil, what was shameful and what was honorable, and always acted accordingly.

48. Sexual relations between an adult and a peri-pubescent child.

49. If that is what Paul is picturing.

8

Is Your God Mean?

The ultimate weakness of violence is that it is a descending spiral,
begetting the very thing it seeks to destroy.
Instead of diminishing evil, it multiplies it . . .
Darkness cannot drive out darkness: only light can do that.
Hate cannot drive out hate: only love can do that.
 —Dr. Martin Luther King Jr.[1]

Your image of God creates you.
—Richard Rohr[2]

ALL OF THE "HOT button" issues we've discussed are subsumed under a
debate about the _nature of God._ The word for this is "ontological." And all
theology really boils down to one big ontological *tension*: Is God primarily
a God of *love*; or primarily a God of *holiness*? It's no use trying to duck
around the question. In the end you'll end up stuck on the horns of *this*
dilemma. Of course the answer is: "He's *both*." And everyone agrees about
that. But there are times when God simply can't be strictly fastidious about

1. King, *Where Do We Go from Here*, 62–3.
2. Rohr, "Toxic Image of God."

both at the same time; one has to give way to the other for God to act in his *relationship* with sinful people.

God is God, and he does what he wants.[3] But it's up to us to *interpret* those actions and make our decisions about him from there. The way people answer this foundational question says a lot more about *them* than it does about God. But since God has left us on Earth as his sole "PR firm,"[4] the way we answer affects how others see him. Therefore, it's actually quite important. Sometimes we have to deal with *ontological questions*, whether we call them that or not. Most modern American Christians aren't prepared to do this, and it shows.

Many American evangelicals and fundamentalists have essentially transformed God into a cosmic Santa Claus. They believe if they ask *hard* enough, and have *enough* faith, God will pony up and give them what they want. Have you heard someone say something like, "I'm going to pray harder about that"; or, "I need to get more people to join in prayer so God will . . ."? It's as if they think if they pray *passionately* enough, or get enough voices to join them, they can convince God to give them something he *doesn't* naturally want to provide. It makes God out to be a *reluctant* genie. This sentiment is at the heart of most modern megachurch belief systems. Yet it's not an idea that bears much scriptural scrutiny.

In the Bible God is presented in two *conflicting* ways. He is either distressingly *holy*:

> I saw the Lord sitting on a throne, high and lofty; and the hem of his robe filled the temple. Seraphs were in attendance above him; each had six wings: with two they covered their faces, and with two they covered their feet, and with two they flew. And one called to another and said: "Holy, holy, holy is the Lord of hosts; the whole earth is full of his glory." The pivots on the thresholds shook at the voices of those who called, and the house filled with smoke. And I said: "Woe is me! I am lost, for I am a man of unclean lips, and I live among a people of unclean lips; yet my eyes have seen the king, the Lord of hosts!"[5]

Or he's presented in nearly polar opposite terms:

---

3. See Psalm 115:3: "Our God is in the heavens; he does whatever he pleases"; and Psalm 135:5–6: "For I know that the Lord is great; our Lord is above all gods. Whatever the Lord pleases he does, in heaven and on earth, in the seas and all deeps."

4. Public relations.

5. Isaiah 6:1–5.

Rejoice with Jerusalem, and be glad for her, all you who love her; rejoice with her in joy, all you who mourn over her—that you may nurse and be satisfied from her consoling breast; that you may drink deeply with delight from her glorious bosom. For thus says the Lord: I will extend prosperity to her like a river, and the wealth of the nations like an overflowing stream; and you shall nurse and be carried on her arm, and dandled on her knees. As a mother comforts her child, so I will comfort you; you shall be comforted in Jerusalem.[6]

These two passages bring us back to our original question: Is God primarily holy and transcendent, approached only with extreme caution, if at all; *or* an ever-imminent mother who longs to hold us close and nurture us with love, protection, and abiding comfort? Both personas are found frequently throughout the Bible. But what is *never* found is an image of God who is *ill disposed* toward us, or *oblivious* to our plights, until we "pray hard enough" (or get enough people to join us in entreaty) to compel his unenthusiastic hand into action. And while myriad examples can be found of *both* God's holiness and love, there are times when both simply cannot *simultaneously* prevail. God has to set one aside and accommodate the other. That's the point we're looking for—because *there* we'll find what is truly at the core of God's being.

Complicating this debate for most evangelical and fundamentalist Christians is their belief that all portions of the Bible are *equal.* Far too many believe that the Bible is intended to be God's "answer book," a spiritual textbook to study, or rulebook to obey. Scripture has been transformed by that belief into a weapon to be used against people who believe differently, instead of a *source* that *invites us to wrestle*[7] with God, and find *healing* for our souls.

Any Christian's approach to the Bible goes a long way in forming his or her conception of God. And a person's understanding of God greatly impacts their attitude toward other people—especially people who are different. Religion, the corporate expression of faith, can greatly reinforce that attitude—for good or ill. *Lex orandi, lex credenda*[8] is a Latin phrase

---

6. Isaiah 66:10–13.

7. The word *Israel* literally means "one who wrestles with God." It was a name of *honor* given to Jacob, and the name applied to the whole nation of Old Testament people who lived in this kind of dynamic tension with God. "Wrestling" does not necessarily imply rebellion, but can be deeply reverent and respectful.

8. Credited to Prosper of Aquitaine, a fourth-century church leader. It is often translated, "As you pray, so you will believe." The idea is that the way we worship forms the way

that addresses this reality. It suggests that the way we pray and worship forms the way we believe. And this is undeniably true. However, it is only half the story. In modern America the way we believe also forms the way we choose to worship.[9] For example, if you don't believe the Lord's Supper imparts anything special, then you'll naturally choose to worship someplace where its seldom celebrated, and you'll likely lobby to minimize how often it takes up time in services. If, however, you consider it a sacrament imparting grace, forgiveness, and a special presence of Jesus, then you're likely to attend somewhere its given a much more prominent place in the community's worship life. The same holds true for everything that's a part (or not a part) of worship. *Lex orandi, lex credenda* is only one half of a cycle, which together with the other half, *lex credendi, lex oranda*, forms a sort of *discipleship cycle*:

Practice forming belief	→	and belief forming practice
(which continues with)		(which repeats with)
belief reinforcing practice	←	practice reinforcing belief

This relentless cycle produces a *weltanschauung*: a holistic worldview. The longer a person remains a part of any particular system of thought and practice, the more deeply engrained both become—that's true whether the system is healthy or unhealthy.

A couple paragraphs back I said that evangelicals and fundamentalists generally believe all parts of the Bible are equal. That might have struck you as an odd thing to say. Some might have even thought that to deny *that* verges on heresy. So let's consider it for a minute. Allow me to pose a couple questions to you: Is Moses as important as Jesus? Obviously all the prophets are important, but are they all equal? Is the book of Hebrews more or less vital to our faith than the weird and exciting book of Revelation? And where do the Gospels fall in the mix? If you could only choose to have either Ephesians or Matthew, which would you pick? . . . Why?

When forced to answer these kinds of questions, most people agree Jesus is more important than Moses and the book of Matthew is more vital than Ephesians. But many Christians' *practice* contradicts that answer. James was on to this two millennia ago when he wrote: "Show me your faith

we eventually grow think theologically.

9. We have an ability to choose which congregations to attend that is unique in history.

without deeds, and I will show you my faith by my deeds."[10] Every church claims to worship Jesus, but many fundamentalist and evangelical congregations *act* like they worship Paul or Moses far *more*. They spend far more time hearing sermons from the New Testament epistles or Old Testament than on Jesus as we see him in the Gospels.

In progressive Protestantism *Jesus is embraced as more important in revealing God than Moses or Paul*. Accordingly, we generally read from the Gospels every week and focus our sermons around him more than in typical evangelical or fundamentalist congregations. Moses and Paul were undoubtedly good guys—saints even. But they were just men who were "inspired" to teach us *about* God. Jesus is the only-begotten Son of God— who descended from heaven to reveal God to us.[11] There are a couple of Scripture passages that make this very clear. Consider: "[Jesus] is the image of the invisible God, the firstborn of all creation";[12] and, "Long ago God spoke to our ancestors in many and various ways by the prophets, but in these last days he has spoken to us by a Son, whom he appointed heir of all things, through whom he also created the worlds. He is the reflection of God's glory and the exact imprint of God's very being."[13] These passages make it clear that Jesus is uniquely qualified to weigh in on matters divine. So if Moses and Jesus, or Jesus and Paul, seem to reflect God differently, then we favor the perspective advanced by Jesus.

Consider this example: in the Old Testament prostitutes were "cut off" from the people as pariahs. Even their money was not supposed to be accepted in the temple.[14] And non-virgin women who married Israelite men under false pretense (of being "pure") were to be stoned to death at their father's front door when their duplicity was discovered.[15] Adulterers were to be put to death as well.[16] However, when Jesus is confronted with a crowd of infuriated men bent on enforcing the Old Testament Law to the letter, this occurs: "The scribes and the Pharisees brought a woman whom had been caught in adultery; and making her stand before all of them, they said to him, 'Teacher, this woman was caught in the very act of committing adultery. Now in the

10. James 2:18.
11. John 6:38.
12. Colossians 1:15.
13. Hebrews 1:1–3.
14. Deuteronomy 23:17–18.
15. Deuteronomy 22:20–21.
16. Leviticus 20:10.

law Moses commanded us to stone such women. Now what do you say?"[17] There should have been *no question* regarding what to do; the Law was clear on the matter. The only real question should have been, "Where's the dude she was caught with?" But that's obviously not how Jesus proceeds. He offers the familiar corrective:

> Jesus bent down and wrote with his finger on the ground. When they kept on questioning him, he straightened up and said to them, "Let anyone among you who is without sin be the first to throw a stone at her." And once again he bent down and wrote on the ground. When they heard it, they went away, one by one, beginning with the elders; and Jesus was left alone with the woman standing before him. Jesus straightened up and said to her, "Woman, where are they? Has no one condemned you?" She said, "No one, sir." And Jesus said, "Neither do I condemn you. Go your way, and from now on do not sin again."[18]

We all love this story of grace and mercy! So who better reflects *who God really is*: Moses and the ancient Torah, or Jesus and this radical departure from those rules? Each of us has to decide for him or herself. Both are in the Bible. But they are contradictory on their face. You can't embrace both at the same time. Either you stone the woman, or you refrain, remembering you have plenty of your own guilt. You can't have both on this one and neither can God. One passage better reflects his *essence*. The other is an imperfect reflection.

The answer should be easy—at least for . . . Christians. Jesus is the very image of the Father;[19] Moses is a pale facsimile. Jesus shows us a different vision of God. That's why all through the Sermon on the Mount he says: "You have heard it said . . . but I say to you . . ." He was radically reforming humanity's conception of God, starting with Israel. He was reinterpreting God for us. God *says* he is full of "steadfast love" all through the Old Testament, but it rarely *looked* like it. In Jesus we can begin to believe it!

I should let you know that I pulled a *fast one* on you. I believe everything I just said. But I built my case on the shakiest foundation I could think of.[20] The story of Jesus' encounter with this woman was very likely *not* in the original Gospel of John. It was added later. In fact, as it begins to be

17. John 8:3–5.

18. John 8:6b–11.

19. Hebrews 1:3.

20. With the exception of the longer ending of Mark, 16:9–19, which was certainly not in the original Gospel.

added to the text of Scripture it shows up in *different* places, until everybody finally settled into including it as the last verse of John 7 and the beginning of chapter 8. Check your Bible and see, but it probably says something like my version of the NRSV: "The most ancient authorities lack 7:53—8:11; other authorities add the passage here or after 7:36 or after 21:25 or after Luke 21:38, with variations of text; some mark the passage as doubtful."[21] Doubtful? That's putting it mildly! It pops up in several different places, and even in a totally different Gospel. But the question for us should be: Does this seem like something Jesus would say and do, based on everything else we know of him? And the obvious answer is "*Yes!*" and that's, undoubtedly, why church leaders began adding it. It *adds* to the church's understanding of God. One can say that this late addition was "inspired" by God, even if it wasn't in the first, second, or tenth edition of John's Gospel.

The God that Jesus speaks of often bears scant resemblance to the God of the Old Testament—especially as he's presented in the books of Exodus, Joshua, and Judges. And that's something theologians from the first century onward reflect on a lot. One of them, Marcion of Sinope, had so much difficulty reconciling the biblical depictions of God that he taught that the deity of the Old Testament was a *completely different being* from the one presented to us by Jesus. Marcion was the first person (we know of) to propose an official canon of what we call the New Testament—though it's different from the one that was finally adopted over a century later. While he affirmed the God presented to us by Christ is the *true God*, that wasn't good enough for most of the pastors and bishops of the early 200s CE to overlook his innovative solution to humanity's evolving understanding of God. He was excommunicated for his beliefs.

Have you ever heard someone refer to the "books" of Isaiah? That's because there are probably *three* different books that have been sewn together as a single text.[22] Generally, each is considered to reflect a different stage of the Babylonian exile: pre-, during, and post-. Very few Old Testament scholars regard the book of Isaiah as written by one man at one time. And it doesn't matter. It's still *inspired* and *profitable* for us. It's profitable because it breathes something of God to us, and we're made better by it. It helps pull us together as communities of people who are seeking God and trying

---

21. National Council of Churches, *Holy Bible: New Revised Standard Version*, 136.

22. Some believe that Isaiah was only actually two books made into one; others believe the book was formed from at least four different authors at four different times.

to breathe his truth to others. Slowly, over centuries and millennia, God's breath has made us better people.

It has also stuck us with some problems. For instance, portions of the Bible that speak of settling the Holy Land include troubling images. They "report" the Israelites practicing genocide in the name of Yahweh. Passages like Deuteronomy 20:10–14, 16:

> When you draw near to a town to fight against it, offer it terms of peace. If it accepts your terms of peace and surrenders to you, then all the people in it shall serve you at forced labor. If it does not submit to you peacefully, but makes war against you, then you shall besiege it; and when the Lord your God gives it into your hand, you shall put all its males to the sword. You may, however, take as your booty the women, the children, livestock, and everything else in the town, all its spoil. You may enjoy the spoil of your enemies, which the Lord your God has given you. . . . As for the towns of these peoples that the Lord your God is giving you as an inheritance, you must not let anything that breathes remain alive.

There's just nothing nice about this text. It is an embarrassment to the God we know though Jesus. If God really ordered the mass genocides of whole populations of people, he is an evil and twisted God like so many of the other Near Eastern gods of that era—and that's the point. The ancient Israelites *projected onto God* stories that reflected his might and power, along with some terrible malevolence, which he never possessed. Those people may have believed God was like them, but he never was. They might have acted terribly in his name, but he never *commanded* or *condoned* any of it.

Read all nine verses of Psalm 137:

> By the rivers of Babylon—there we sat down and there we wept when we remembered Zion. On the willows there we hung up our harps. For there our captors asked us for songs, and our tormentors asked for mirth, saying, "Sing us one of the songs of Zion!" How could we sing the Lord's song in a foreign land? If I forget you, O Jerusalem, let my right hand wither! Let my tongue cling to the roof of my mouth, if I do not remember you, if I do not set Jerusalem above my highest joy. Remember, O Lord, against the

Edomites the day of Jerusalem's fall, how they said, "Tear it down! Tear it down! Down to its foundations!" O daughter Babylon, you devastator! Happy shall they be who pay you back what you have done to us! Happy shall they be who take your little ones and dash them against the rock!

You read that right. The psalmist celebrates, in a holy psalm to God, bashing babies' brains out on rocks. Many—perhaps most—Christians are familiar with the beginning of this psalm: the lament about Jerusalem and the bit about hanging their harps on the willows. But very few know the last verse of this psalm is in the Bible. The idea of celebrating such hate in holy song is simply beyond the pale for most Christians. No one I know would *celebrate* intentionally harming babies. But. There. It. Is. In. The. Bible. Horrifying!

Which is, no doubt, why we usually skip that verse when we read this psalm in church. We have met Jesus, and we know this sort of thing is *not* OK with God because of him. He teaches us: "For God so loved the world that he gave his only Son, so that everyone who believes in him may not perish but may have eternal life. Indeed, God did not send the Son into the world to condemn the world, but in order that the world might be saved through him."[23] God's *love* for *all* people is stronger than his ontological holiness. So great is that love that Jesus, the Son of God, pursued us into death so that he could bring us into divine life.

One of the most common theories in America about *why* Jesus had to die on the cross is called the "penal substitutionary atonement" view (PSA).[24] An archbishop of Canterbury called Anselm, who lived from 1033–1109, developed it.[25] It is beyond the scope of my purposes to discuss this at length, but the PSA theory introduced emerging legal concepts *into* theology that hadn't existed prior to Anselm.[26] Basically, he taught that God was so holy that he couldn't simply forgive sin without killing someone. Since the death of sinful people didn't assuage God's bloodlust, he needed a sinless person to die in our place. It maps out like this: *death* is the *penalty* necessary to satisfy God's holiness; *Christ* volunteered to be our *substitute* because only he could meet this demand; this satisfied God's need to kill (sacrifice) someone, for *atonement* to occur. This theory makes God a fiend,

23. John 3:16–17.

24. See chapter 2.

25. He was born in Aosta in Italy and served as a Benedictine abbot in Bec, France, before being elevated to bishop.

26. This is another example of an anachronism altering long-established theology.

who kills his Son so he can accept you and me into his presence—and bring us to heaven when we die.

I understand that most American evangelicals and fundamentalists think the Bible says this is what happened and *why* God did it. But it isn't nearly that simple. If it were it wouldn't have taken over a thousand years for pastors, priests, and bishops to figure it out! For the first millennia of church history pastors believed that death was the fruit of sin—they were linked. Sin essentially *was* death; it killed our relationships: with God, with other humans, and with creation as a whole. Sin wasn't thought of as an *ontological* reality on its own. Sin doesn't exist in itself. It is like the cold, or the dark. Those things have no ontological reality of their own either. They are the *lack* of something. Cold is a lack of heat. The same goes for the dark: it's lack of light. Sin is a lack of *being like God*—of reflecting him. It brings us to death—which is lack of being alive or of having the life (breath) of God.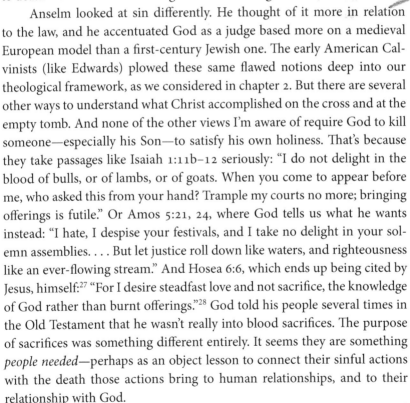

Anselm looked at sin differently. He thought of it more in relation to the law, and he accentuated God as a judge based more on a medieval European model than a first-century Jewish one. The early American Calvinists (like Edwards) plowed these same flawed notions deep into our theological framework, as we considered in chapter 2. But there are several other ways to understand what Christ accomplished on the cross and at the empty tomb. And none of the other views I'm aware of require God to kill someone—especially his Son—to satisfy his own holiness. That's because they take passages like Isaiah 1:11b–12 seriously: "I do not delight in the blood of bulls, or of lambs, or of goats. When you come to appear before me, who asked this from your hand? Trample my courts no more; bringing offerings is futile." Or Amos 5:21, 24, where God tells us what he wants instead: "I hate, I despise your festivals, and I take no delight in your solemn assemblies. . . . But let justice roll down like waters, and righteousness like an ever-flowing stream." And Hosea 6:6, which ends up being cited by Jesus, himself:[27] "For I desire steadfast love and not sacrifice, the knowledge of God rather than burnt offerings."[28] God told his people several times in the Old Testament that he wasn't really into blood sacrifices. The purpose of sacrifices was something different entirely. It seems they are something *people needed*—perhaps as an object lesson to connect their sinful actions with the death those actions bring to human relationships, and to their relationship with God.

27. Matthew 9:13 and 12:7.

28. See also 1 Samuel 15:22.

Jesus makes this point in Matthew 9 when he dines with Matthew the tax collector. The religious elite are outraged that Jesus stands (or sits) in solidarity with a traitor.[29] Jesus points out that it is the sick who need healing. He suggests that God rejoices in works of forgiveness and mercy more than pious sacrifices and self-righteous exclusivity. The sacrificial work of Jesus had a lot more to do with showing us the kind of life we're supposed to live: "If any want to become my followers, let them deny themselves and take up their cross daily and follow me."[30] His sacrifice wasn't primarily about sating God's imagined bloodlust.

The psalmist writes: "The fear of the Lord is the beginning of wisdom; all those who practice it have a good understanding. His praise endures forever."[31] The word translated "fear" in this verse, *yirat*, does *not* generally denote terror or trepidation, but rather a deep and abiding respect. "Reverence" would probably be a better choice when translating this word today. In fact the word is frequently translated that way in other passages. True respect for God doesn't leave one paralyzed with dread, but energizes us with peace and trust. It drives us to act like him, to the extent that's possible. A proper conception of God views him as abundantly trustworthy and devotedly loving. As 1John 4:16–18 explains: "God is love, and those who abide in love abide in God, and God abides in them. Love has been perfected among us in this: that we may have boldness on the day of judgment, because as he is, so are we in this world. There is no fear in love, but perfect love casts out fear; for fear has to do with punishment, and whoever fears has not reached perfection in love." His holiness is a part of who he is, but it is tempered and put in check by his love of us. His love is of a *sacrificial* quality. He subjects his perfection to his love in his dealings with humanity. Therefore he willingly sacrifices his holiness in order to have an ongoing and authentic relationship with people who are not perfect.

When the many passages of the Bible are taken together, and *filtered through Jesus*, they reveal a *different God* from the one created by those who believe God is so holy he can't look on sin. Habakkuk thought much the same thing, and he wrote that accusation down about God: "Your eyes are too pure to behold evil, and you cannot look on wrongdoing."[32] But it wasn't true then (as becomes obvious in the book), and it isn't true now. God's heart breaks as he sees humanity's greed, cruelty, and baseness toward his

29. Which is how tax collectors were regarded.
30. Luke 9:23.
31. Psalm 111:10.
32. Habakkuk 1:13.

creation and especially toward other people. His love drives him to enter this world and work with us to end it and heal its effects.

Violence and retributive "eye for an eye" morality are insufficient to do that work. Only self-sacrifice and serving others can make amends. Love, not holiness, is the answer. In fact, true love is the only thing that can hope to produce holiness in this world. Micah 6:8: "O mortal, what is good; and what does the Lord require of you but to do justice, and to love kindness, and to walk humbly with your God." There is nothing of God's transcendent holiness there. It's all about being a decent person and having mercy toward those who have messed up in some way . . . and being humble before God because no one actually has any right to brag or feel superior to other people. Maybe Jewel has it right: "In the end only kindness matters."[33]

One more thing: God's *wrath*. Many evangelicals and fundamentalists believe it's being poured out in the world today to *punish* human waywardness. Pat Robertson famously claimed Hurricane Katrina, which killed 1,836 people, was the direct result of sinfulness in New Orleans. He suggests abortion was the underlying cause.[34] Of course, anyone can play this game. Rabbi Ovadia Yosef said the storm was punishment on George W. Bush for failing to give *more* support to Israel.[35] Louis Farrakhan claimed it was God's wrath for America's racism.[36] And Abu Musab Al-Zarqawi of Al-Qaeda announced that it was an answer to the prayers of the oppressed.[37]

The connection can even be perilously tangential:

Fred Phelps Jr. (@WBCFredJr):

OK Thunder's Durant flips God by praising fag Collins. God smashes OK. You do the math. #GodH8sFags #FagsDoom-Nations #FearGod #GodH8sU

9:47 PM – May 20, 2013

33. Jewel,"Hands."
34. Robertson, *The 700 Club*, September 12, 2005.
35. As cited by Dyson, *Come Hell or High Water*, 223.
36. Ibid., 178–202.
37. Al-Zarqawi, "Katrina an Answer to Prayers.."

Westboro Baptist Church's Fred Phelps Jr. blamed (via tweet) a devastating tornado that ripped through Moore, Oklahoma, on May 20, 2013, resulting in the deaths of 24 and the total destruction 1,150 homes, on the town's supposed support of Jason Collins, an openly gay NBA player. Collins had no connection to Moore, or even Oklahoma; another player, Kevin Durant, an Oklahoma City player, voiced his *support* for Collins . . . and voilà God smites a nearby town. Presumably, destroying Oklahoma City was too tall an order for Westboro's God, so he zapped a suburb instead. Why God didn't devastate Boston or Washington, DC (the cities for whom Collins actually played) remains a mystery. It's all so ludicrous. And so sad!

God doesn't send storms as punishment; and he never did. I know the story of Sodom and Gomorrah. I'm conversant with Noah and his flood. I know the things the Israelites are supposed to have faced for their whining: snakes, earthquakes, and devastating military losses. But I don't believe those stories happened quite as we have them in the Bible. That is, they are not *historically* true events. They're stories the people who wrote them may have *believed* were true for the reasons they recorded. But they never happened, certainly not as a result of God's uncontrollable anger, or vindictive holiness. They are cautionary tales. They are *inspired* and were important for the time they were written. But they serve no particularly good purpose for us today, except to show where we have come from.

Jesus shows us God differently—and it's not God who has changed; *we have*. God is not in the smiting-whole-cities, or smiting-individuals business.[38] *He never was.* The idea of God indiscriminately harming or killing people and destroying homes, schools and business warps people's conception of God as the loving Father of the whole world. It's an image that also serves to twist some Christian brothers and sisters into the same mold. That image of God creates the possibility of boorish disciples who can spew hate and judgment toward people who are different from them. And the church is rife with this carnage!

God is a God of *love*—he *is* love. Love casts out fear, and acts boldly to unite people into community, and to unite them with God. Love calls us to

38. See Luke 13:1–5: "At that very time there were some present who told him about the Galileans whose blood Pilate had mingled with their sacrifices. He asked them, 'Do you think that because these Galileans suffered in this way they were worse sinners than all other Galileans? No, I tell you; but unless you repent, you will all perish as they did. Or those eighteen who were killed when the tower of Siloam fell on them—do you think that they were worse offenders than all the others living in Jerusalem? No, I tell you; but unless you repent, you will all perish just as they did.'"

stand in solidarity with outcasts and the disenfranchised—with "sinners." Love sacrifices of itself to bless its beloved, to the point of death! The church needs to reclaim *this* initiative. We need to be willing, like Jesus, to risk "skirting" (or breaking) more of the *letters* of the Law, to better fulfill its spirit.[39] We should be compelled by the grace and mercy of Jesus to bring the restorative love of God to those who most need it. This is something that can be done on a daily basis, through the most ordinary of actions, even offering cups of cold water to those who thirst.[40]

39. Romans 2:28–29; 2 Corinthians 3:6.
40. Matthew 10:42.

9

Let's Go to Hell

What is hell? Hell is oneself.
Hell is alone, the other figures in it
Merely projections.

—T. S. Eliot[1]

All hope abandon, ye who enter here!

—Dante Alighieri[2]

ONE OF THE GREATEST powers the church has ever laid claim to is the authority to consign the souls of others to a conscious eternity in the torments of a perpetually burning underworld called "hell." The evangelical and fundamentalist wing of the Protestant church frequently pronounces that her enemies and critics are destined for this place. They often suggest that anyone who doesn't believe exactly *as they teach* will join them there. But going to "hell" might turn out to be more difficult than popularly believed! That's because the modern American notion of hell is derived far more from Dante's *Inferno* than it is from the Bible. Most everyone who's studied the development of the theories of hell, freely admits that our

1. Eliot, *Cocktail Party*, 98.
2. Alighieri, *Inferno*, 27.

modern concept of perdition has very little basis in the Old Testament. In its pages people who die are presented as going to "the Pit," or *Sheol*. It's a non-discriminatory sort of place, inhabited by both good and evil. The Hebrew words are sometimes translated simply as "the grave" or "the dead." And that's a lot more accurate translation of the Hebrew terms than the word "hell." King David writes: "To you, O Lord, I cried, and to the Lord I made supplication: 'What profit is there in my death, if I go down to the Pit? Will the dust praise you? Will it tell of your faithfulness? Hear, O Lord, and be gracious to me! O Lord, be my helper!'"[3] This poem obviously reflects the common Old Testament–era belief that when someone dies they descend to some state of unconsciousness in the grave. This is very different from what we're used to thinking about the afterlife.

Several dozen passages could be marshaled to demonstrate the pervasive Old Testament belief that one was essentially comatose in death. Consider: "Turn, O Lord, save my life; deliver me for the sake of your steadfast love. For in death there is no remembrance of you; in Sheol who can give you praise?";[4] or: "For Sheol cannot thank you, death cannot praise you; those who go down to the Pit cannot hope for your faithfulness."[5] The list could go on and on.

In the Old Testament no one thought about living on in a conscious state with God, or apart from him in some sort of torment. There are a few hints at a universal resurrection . . . some day. But that's all a bit vague and reflects the theology of Israel after they had come into contact with the Greeks. Besides *Sheol*, there are a couple of other Hebrew words that refer to the place of the dead: *Abbaddon*, which means "ruin";[6] *Bor*, often translated as "pit"[7]; and *Shakhat*, meaning "corruption."[8] Most Israelites believed that when a person died they were buried in a pit/grave and their consciousness was rendered asleep or something akin to that.[9]

3. Psalm 30:8–10.

4. Psalm 6:4–5.

5. Isaiah 38:18.

6. Psalm 88:11; Job 28:22.

7. Isaiah 14:15; Ezekiel 26:20.

8. Ezekiel 28:8.

9. There is one exception in 1 Samuel 28, where King Saul has the witch of Endor conjure up the dead prophet Samuel. No one seems more surprised than her when he arrives! Other than that, people who are dead are dead. They do nothing, and think nothing. They don't praise God. They aren't in bliss; nor are they seen in torment. They are in some sort of *stasis*, at best.

That's so different from what most Americans are taught today about death and the hereafter. And that should raise a question: What has led us to modify the traditional Old Testament view of death? As we've seen, our understanding of many things has changed since Old Testament times—Jesus intentionally altered a lot of what Moses had taught. But the answer to why our belief about *hell* has evolved isn't simple to answer. Most of what we believe about "hell" does come from Jesus—and mostly from things he said in the Gospel of Matthew. But, it turns out, it doesn't come to us *directly* from Jesus; it takes a side trip to pick up baggage from the medieval era. In other words, Jesus doesn't *actually say* what we *think* he says. Quite the opposite, in fact. And that's a problem!

Each time Jesus refers to "hell" in Matthew the Greek word he uses is *Gehenna*. This comes from the Hebrew phrase "the Valley of the Son of Hinnom." It's a place just southwest of Jerusalem. A bit of historic perspective is essential to understanding what the people of Jesus' day would have thought when *they* heard it referenced. This site was where the ancient Israelites had worshipped other deities, including Baal and Molech—it is where they had "caused their children to pass through the fire."[10] In more direct words, it's where they had sacrificed their children as burnt offerings to various Canaanite gods in 700–600 BCE. You can read about this in 2 Chronicles 28 and 33, and you can see the resulting attitude toward the place centuries later in Jeremiah 7 and 19. Suffice it to say that later Jews thought the place to be cursed beyond redemption, or even haunted.

The people of Jerusalem burned trash there, especially human and animal refuse and the bodies of dead animals and crucified malefactors. It was used as an interment site for cremains for centuries, and in 70 CE the Tenth Legion of Rome cremated masses of people in this place, when they demolished Jerusalem. While the Romans used the site *after* Jesus' lifetime, their actions had *already occurred* by the time the Gospel of Matthew was written. In the Jewish Mishnah[11] it's recorded that people who had done terrible things would often go to Gehenna to *atone* for their sins—something like purgatory for the living. People might spend up to a year in Gehenna purging their guilt and penitently seeking to reestablish human relationships.[12]

---

10. 2 Kings 16:3; 17:17 (KJV). See also Jeremiah 19:5 and Ezekiel 20:26, 31.

11. The earliest major redaction of Jewish oral traditions that were written down for rabbinic studies—a sort of commentary on the major themes of the Old Testament.

12. This belief is recorded a bit after Jesus' time, but was practiced well before the

When Jesus uses the word *Gehenna* he is evoking all kinds of emotional content and historic context. What he is definitely *not* evoking are thoughts of demons roasting unbelievers in a fiery pit somewhere in the center of the Earth. First-century Jews would not have pictured the same images *we conjure up* when we hear the word "hell." And this is very important for us realize. "Hell," as we conceive of it, is an invention of medieval thought—most especially a famous poem called *The Inferno*, written between 1308 and 1320 CE as a part of an epic poem called *The Divine Comedy* by Dante Alighieri.[13]

The closest Jesus comes to depicting a hell like we're accustomed to is the parable of Lazarus and the rich man.[14] This story is one of the few that is found *only* in Luke's Gospel, which is notable because Luke was not written for a Jewish or Palestinian audience—but rather to Greeks, who already had a long-established tradition of an underworld afterlife, called Hades. In Luke's recounting of this parable we still don't have anything approaching modern ideas of heaven and hell. There is no heaven at all, but rather "Abraham's Bosom,"[15] a place in close proximity to the area of torment mentioned in the story. The people in the two disparate parts could see one another and speak to each other. The Greek idea of Hades is assimilated by the writer of Luke, and altered to include a pleasant place and a different portion for torment.

The real problem with using this story to inform our concept of the afterlife is that the parable is *not* intended to teach us details about the *spiritual experiences* of the dead. It is a *morality* story. The rich man is unnamed[16] because he is forgotten after death. He had enjoyed the best life had to offer and he failed to take care of even one poor man who had lain at his very door. He was self-centered and uncaring. And after death, Jesus presents him as having no comfort. Every indication is that this wealthy man would have been regarded as a *decent fellow* by normal human standards; he'd be admired in modern American society as a *success*. He was a rich, Jewish man in first-century Israel. Others would likely have regarded him as respectable or even enviable. And *that's* the point. Jesus

---

first century.

13. Alighieri, *Inferno*.

14. Luke 16:19–31.

15. KJV.

16. There is similar motif in Ruth 4, where Ruth's closer kinsman redeemer's name is forgotten; he is referred to as "Mr. So-and-So." Only Boaz is named.

uses this ideal man as a trope for something radical and unforeseen. He places *this guy* in "torment." And he presents poor, sick Lazarus—sometime companion of dogs—as the hero in the story. It should go without saying that this was extraordinarily shocking, and likely salacious, to the typical Jew (or anyone!). The heinous *crime* of the rich man, which landed him in "hell": complacency, *lack of care and concern* for a poor diseased man lying near his home. Nothing else. That was *sufficient* to visit God's punishment upon him.[17] God makes it abundantly clear in the Bible that we all have a moral responsibility to care for the poor and the sick, the widow and the orphan. Jesus' brother, James, puts it this way: "Religion[18] that is pure and undefiled before God, the Father, is this: to care for orphans and widows in their distress, and to keep oneself unstained by the world."[19] Failing to practice proper care for the unfortunate among us, individually and as part of a group (church), is the *damning* fault of the rich man in the parable. Jesus' hearers would have been blown away by that. That's the real point of the story—not the *incidental* depiction of "hell." It's intended metaphorically to drive God's displeasure home to the hearers and readers of the parable.

The other Gospel passage that adds the most to a discussion of both "hell" and the actions that get one sent there is found in Matthew 25. This is the seminal passage of the great Judgment Day:

> When the Son of Man comes in his glory, and all the angels with him, then he will sit on the throne of his glory. All the nations will be gathered before him, and he will separate people one from another as a shepherd separates the sheep from the goats, and he will put the sheep at his right hand and the goats at the left. Then the king will say to those at his right hand, "Come, you that are blessed by my Father, inherit the kingdom prepared for you from the foundation of the world; for I was hungry and you gave me food, I was thirsty and you gave me something to drink, I was a stranger and you welcomed me, I was naked and you gave me clothing, I was sick and you took care of me, I was in prison and you visited me." . . . Then he will say to those at his left hand, "You that are accursed, depart from me into the eternal fire prepared

17. This is nearly the same thing that Sodom was actually guilty of as explained by Ezekiel 16:49–50. He is guilty on a personal level of the same thing the Sodomite society was guilty of collectively. Both are judged by "fire," the transformative element of the ancient world.

18. "Religion" is not a dirty word in the Bible. It is an *expectation*—the way we worship God along with others, which the Bible praises.

19. James 1:27.

for the devil and his angels; for I was hungry and you gave me no food, I was thirsty and you gave me nothing to drink, I was a stranger and you did not welcome me, naked and you did not give me clothing, sick and in prison and you did not visit me." Then they also will answer, "Lord, when was it that we saw you hungry or thirsty or a stranger or naked or sick or in prison, and did not take care of you?" Then he will answer them, "Truly I tell you, just as you did not do it to one of the least of these, you did not do it to me." And these will go away into eternal punishment, but the righteous into eternal life.[20]

In the parallel passage in Revelation the unjust are sent to the "Lake of Fire":

Then I saw a great white throne and the one who sat on it; the earth and the heaven fled from his presence, and no place was found for them. And I saw the dead, great and small, standing before the throne, and books were opened. Also another book was opened, the book of life. And the dead were judged according to their works, as recorded in the books. And the sea gave up the dead that were in it, Death and Hades gave up the dead that were in them, and all were judged according to what they had done. Then Death and Hades were thrown into the lake of fire. This is the second death, the lake of fire; and anyone whose name was not found written in the book of life was thrown into the lake of fire.[21]

A couple of things here inform our understanding of "hell." Judgment is always seen as *corporate*. Jesus judges everyone at the same time. That's why the church has traditionally referred to this as the "Day of Judgment" or the "Last Day." Additionally, while the emphasis of most "Bible-believing"[22] churches seems to be fixed primarily on the "hereafter" and "getting people to heaven when they die," Jesus is a lot more focused on making a positive difference in the here-and-now.

Also, note Jesus doesn't ask if the people had "invited him into their hearts." He asks them if they fed the poor and cared for the needy. Both of the great passages dealing with the afterlife and judgment speak of our *works* being the thing evaluated. I realize that Paul says: "For by grace you

20. Matthew 25:31–36, 41–45.

21. Revelation 20:11–15.

22. Many fundamental and evangelical congregations *self-style* their congregations with this term, apparently differentiating themselves from other churches that are "Bible doubting" (snarky, I know).

have been saved through faith, and this is not your own doing; it is the gift of God—not the result of works, so that no one may boast. For we are what he has made us, created in Christ Jesus for good works, which God prepared beforehand to be our way of life."[23] But note, we are made into a new creation in Christ to do "good works."

The theological separation of faith from works in evangelicalism and fundamentalism has done great harm to the cause of Christ. Jesus did not come just to save our disembodied souls when we die. He came to build his kingdom on Earth, among us, now. Jesus wants us to live the Beatitudes. He wants us to join the marginalized, and lend them our privilege—use *our* power to make *their* lives better. This is implicit in the Lord's Prayer when we say, "Thy kingdom come." He desires each of us to play our part in making that kingdom an earthly reality. But all this has little to do with "hell"—except that *not doing it* seems to be what gets you sent there!

On the Last Day, Death and Hades will give up their dead. All people will be brought before the king of creation—Jesus the Messiah—to be judged according to what they have and haven't done. Those rejected by Christ will be cast into a place called the "Lake of Fire." This place is also referred to as "the second death."[24]

As we've discussed, death doesn't ontologically exist. It's the *absence* of life. So if being cast into the Lake of Fire is the *second* death, we ought to consider the *first* death more closely. In this context, it is when the soul leaves the body the first time, when the person "gives up the ghost." After the death of a "lost" person—one bound for the Lake of Fire—a couple of things happen: the physical body is buried, cremated, committed to the deep—whatever; and the soul goes to Hades or the Pit. On the Last Day the body and soul will be reunited to stand before Jesus[25] to be sentenced—cast into the Lake of Fire, in their case. *This* is the second death.

We're generally told that hell, or the Lake of Fire, is the place that non-Christians spend "eternity." And by that evangelicals and fundamentalists generally mean *temporal* eternity—day after day after day, forever and ever. It's a place of fire and torment. It's dark and hot and there's no

23. Ephesians 2:8–10.

24. Revelation 20:6, 14. Note in verse 6 the "second death" holds no power over the "blessed."

25. In fact all people may arrive at this Great Judgment simultaneously. When a person leaves the body, they also leaves linear time. It is quite possible that the thief on the cross in Luke 23, Stephen the first martyr, you and I, and people who die two thousand years from now will "arrive" at the Last Day at the same moment.

relief. It just goes on and on, burning and tormenting the souls of those who didn't accept Jesus during their life. They may have been married to a great Christian who shared Christ's love with them thousands of times in gentle and respectful ways; or they may have heard it once, from a missionary; or they may have gone to parochial school and been molested by a teacher; or they may have grown up in a "Christian" home where they were subject to horrible abuse (secretly) yet lauded at church as a "perfect family"; or they may have been exposed to the "gospel" at gunpoint during colonialism. Not everyone hears the gospel in ways that *evoke* a positive response. Some people are exposed to a "gospel" that is no gospel at all. It is offered as exploitation. Or sometimes it's all mixed up with abuse and evil that so taints the gospel it's not recognizable as "good news" at all. But in most evangelicals' and fundamentalists' minds, if a person heard the simple *facts about Jesus* once, they're "accountable." And rejection means they're going to roast in the flames of hell, quite literally . . . forever.[26]

This is a flawed understanding of hell on several levels. It misunderstands: what constitutes the gospel, what's *required* to avoid hell, the *temporal quality* of the place, and the idea that Christ and his gospel can *only* come to a person in physical life. Let's consider these one at a time. Most American evangelicals and fundamentalists believe in the relatively modern notion of "accepting Jesus into one's heart as a personal savior." They believe that a person must pray a "Sinners' Prayer" of one sort or another. Usually this means they tell God they're a sinner and seek his forgiveness by inviting Jesus into their heart. Most believe that *this* is the gospel. The "good news" is the simple fact that Jesus died (in your place) so you can go to heaven when you die. Accepting these facts, and telling God you believe them, is the gospel John the Baptizer and Jesus went about sharing with people. It's the message the apostles picked up and spread across the world. However, this style of "salvation" is actually quite new. It came on the scene with Jonathan Edwards in the eighteenth century. This view of salvation didn't exist in any other time or place in church history, until Edwards petrified two congregations[27] with his "Sinners in the Hands of an Angry God" sermon. Shortly after, oodles of people were publically accepting Jesus into their hearts[28] and getting saved from moribund Anglicanism. The political

26. I'm simply going to ignore the eternal plight of those who never heard about Jesus, because even evangelicals and fundamentalists agree that is pure speculation.

27. One in Northampton, Massachusetts, the other in Enfield, Connecticut.

28. And actually I'm vastly overstating this in *their* favor—even Jonathan Edwards

climate was ripe for this rejection of the ways of the "Old World"—especially England. The intellectual climate was too. The Enlightenment was teaching people to reject superstition and embrace "modern thought." For Edward's hearers this meant casting off faith in infant baptism, and replacing it with a personal and intellectual choice to become a Christian. Instead of trusting the church and the spooky sacraments, divines of the day were beginning to preach the novel idea that everyone needed to make a personal, intellectual choice to identify with Jesus.

Of course, it was far more natural for people of former eras to conceive of kingdoms where sovereign kings ruled people with only nominal consent. In fact, it was easier for them to conceptualize two warring kings both laying claim to the same set of people than it is for us. Many of them had experienced it in Europe! The idea that the kingdom of God is joined only through personal acceptance of Jesus into one's heart was a radical innovation.[29] And it is the stuff of the Enlightenment. However, "faith," as it is presented in the Bible, is essentially the same thing as trust. And trust isn't something you say or do one time following a scary sermon about hell and a terrifying, malevolent God. _Trust is a lifelong relationship lived out in love._ Trust is exactly the opposite of what Edwards was building on. He was building on _fear._ Jesus nowhere requires his followers to parrot acceptance of seven or eight "key beliefs" in a coached prayer following a sermon where people have quite literally been threatened with eternal hellfire and torture. Instead, he invites people to experience the grace of his kingdom reality—he urges us to live our lives under a different kind of reign. And he wants us to invite others into this "upside-down" reality too. In _this_ concept of salvation, God is looking to get people _into_ his kingdom, not keep them out with lawyer tricks and small print.

That brings us to the notion of the temporal reality of hell. Many theologians reject the idea that hell lasts forever and ever, day after day after day. There is a different understanding of "eternal" from the _temporal_ kind. Something can be "eternal" in its _finality_ as well. For example, if I place a piece of paper into a fire, it's gone. Forever.[30] And that brings us

---

didn't do what is most common in evangelical and fundamentalist churches today, though he moved American theology in that direction.

29. Anabaptists and others had taught some of these ideas, but the views had never become popular on this scale.

30. I know the modern laws of physics will say otherwise, but Jesus wasn't speaking into a culture with Newtonian physics, let alone quantum physics. He was speaking to first-century people.

squarely back to the notion of the "Lake of Fire." The Bible doesn't consign
the souls of the lost to a "lake of formaldehyde" or some other *preservative*.
It consigns them to the most *destructive force* they were aware of: fire.[31] In
fact, fire was more than just destructive; it was the *transformative* element.
In many ancient cultures, the world was viewed as being made up of four
elements: water, earth, air, and fire. The creation myth of Genesis 1 deals
with the three constructive of these elements in great detail:

> "In the beginning when God created the heavens and the earth,
> the earth was a formless void and darkness covered the face of
> the deep, while a wind from God swept over the face of the wa-
> ters . . . And God said, "Let there be a dome in the midst of the wa-
> ters, and let it separate the waters from the waters." So God made
> the dome and separated the waters that were under the dome from
> the waters that were above the dome. And it was so. God called the
> dome Sky. And there was evening and there was morning, the sec-
> ond day. And God said, "Let the waters under the sky be gathered
> together into one place, and let the dry land appear." And it was so.
> God called the dry land Earth, and the waters that were gathered
> together he called Seas. And God saw that it was good.[32]

God shows his dominion over the rudimentary element of *water*, which he
demonstrates by drawing the atmosphere ("waters above") from the water
below; he continues to reveal his dominance by drawing the *earth* from water. God births our world (sky, land, and sea) from primordial water. That
leaves only fire—the destructive or transformative[33] element—absent. It's
found at the End, again under God's control, serving his purpose: burning
away the souls of the lost—perhaps even transforming them into the other
three elements.[34]

Some church fathers and modern scholars[35] believe in "annihilation-
ism." They think the people judged in Matthew 25 and Revelation 20 are
burned up—*once for all*, not day after day. They *cease to exist* after the Judg-

---

31. One of the four classical Greek elements that were thought to comprise the basis
of everything in the universe: earth, water, air and fire. Aristotle added a fifth: ether,
which made up things above the celestial dome, in what we would call "outer space."

32. Genesis 1:1–2, 6–10.

33. When something is burned it leaves ash (earth), water, and emits smoke (air)—
the other three elements.

34. Thoughts which would be consistent with the views of Heraclitus (535–575 BCE)
and Plato (427–347 BCE).

35. John Stott, F. F. Bruce, and C. S. Lewis.

ment. This is what is meant by "the second death." Most of them believed that very few people (perhaps as few as 1–2 percent or *less*) would actually face this end. Many other church fathers favored a stricter form of universalism—the belief that literally all people would be saved in the end.

All early pastors and bishops knew that Jesus had accomplished something spectacular in his death and resurrection. *He savaged hell.*[36] He wholly defeated sin, death, and the devil. *Christus Victor!* This is why art depicting him in resurrection glory frequently includes the Greek word *nike*—"victory"! For most of them that divine victory spanned all of space and time, and subsumes even those who don't "accept Jesus into their hearts" in their lifetimes. Because of this, men like Ambrose, Anthony, Arnobius, Athanasius, Basil, Bardaisan, Chrysostom, Clement of Alexandria, Didymus, Diodore of Tarsus, Gregory of Nazianzus, Gregory of Nyssa, Ignatius, Irenaeus, Jerome, John of Jerusalem, Justin Martyr, Macrina, Methodius, Origin, Pamphilus Martyr, Theodore of Mopsuestia, and Theophilus of Antioch taught something called "universalism."[37] It teaches that *all* people will eventually be saved. They believe if almighty God and king Jesus truly want all to be saved,[38] they will be. After all, when a king conquers a land, all the inhabitants become his *subjects*, whether they like it or not.[39] Even Augustine admitted that a strong case for universalism could be made from the Scriptures, though he never personally adopted it. Their understanding of Jesus as Messiah—king of the universe—and his gospel proclamation in the place of the dead[40] bought them to this conclusion. When a king conquers a land, he often has some help from within the country. He also meets with a good deal of opposition. But the vast *majority* of people play very little active roles whatsoever. They go to work or farm their fields and hope the actual fighting stays away from them. They just keep their heads

36. Christian theology has historically referred to this event as the "Harrowing of Hell."

37. Someone may argue that one or the other of the men in this list was actually a soft Annihilationist; meaning, as explained above, they believed very few people would actually be cast into the Lake of Fire. I have tried to be accurate, but admit that due to the changing beliefs of most of the early Fathers, I may have lumped someone who believed 99 percent of people would be saved in with those who believed 100 percent would. I apologize if that is the case—But the point remains the same: their beliefs were radically different from most evangelicals and fundamentalists who suggest that *most* people will end up in hell forever.

38. 2 Peter 3:9.

39. See Isaiah 25.

40. 1 Peter 3:19.

down and their mouths shut and wait for it to be over. It's actually no different on the religious or spiritual front. Christians, especially those who are passionate in their faith, are those who are helping God take control of this world. Conversely, there are a few who work hard in opposition. But the vast majority of people from Jesus until now are ambivalent about the whole thing. They aren't especially against God, but neither are they exclusively for him. They are just living their lives and hoping not to get caught up in any cosmic struggle. So what happens to these people on the Last Day?

Most evangelicals and fundamentalists consign them to an eternal hell. But, to stick with our original metaphor of a king seizing new lands: after establishing his reign in the new locale, most kings generally offer the opportunity for former enemies to swear allegiance. They also generally accept obeisance after the fact. As for those who were ambivalent, monarchs usually accept pledges of loyalty in arrears. I believe God will act similarly. I suggest that most people will "get saved" postmortem—after death. That list of ancient church heavyweights above—most of them teach that the majority of humans will actually accept Jesus' kingship after they die. They take 1 Peter 3:18–22 seriously:

> Christ also suffered for sins once for all, the righteous for the unrighteous, in order to bring you to God. He was put to death in the flesh, but made alive in the spirit, in which also he went and made a proclamation to the spirits in prison, who in former times did not obey, when God waited patiently in the days of Noah, during the building of the ark, in which a few, that is, eight persons, were saved through water. And baptism, which this prefigured, now saves you—not as a removal of dirt from the body, but as an appeal to God for a good conscience, through the resurrection of Jesus Christ, who has gone into heaven and is at the right hand of God, with angels, authorities, and powers made subject to him.

Jesus preaches to dead people's souls in "hell." In Jesus' day these kinds of proclamations were announcements of a new reality. They were official. They didn't require one to accept them. No one cared if you believed them in your heart. They simply were. When Jesus or John the Baptizer proclaim the "gospel" or "good news," they are very intentionally employing the term as representatives of another kingdom, one at war with Caesar and imperial Rome, metaphors for this fallen world. Jesus' kingdom is at war with Satan's established kingdom of sin and death. It is a message at odds with the reality the forces of Satan daily try to fool us into believing. The gospel proclamation of Jesus carries all the power of the king it represents. It doesn't depend on the will or acceptance of the *hearer*. It is solely sufficient according to the power of the one who *sent* the message.

When Jesus descended to "hell" to proclaim his message—gospel—it had the power to fully accomplish what it claimed . . . as long as the king (God) and his general (Jesus) could back it up. Ambrose, Anthony, Arnobius, Athanasius, Basil, Bardaisan, Chrysostom, Clement of Alexandria, Didymus, Diodore of Tarsus, Gregory of Nazianzus, Gregory of Nyssa, Ignatius, Irenaeus, Jerome, John of Jerusalem, Justin Martyr, Macrina, Methodius, Origin, Pamphilus Martyr, Theodore of Mopsuestia, and Theophilus of Antioch believed he could. I share their opinion. When Jesus makes his gospel proclamation in the place of the dead it offers the promise of salvation to all who hear it. When Jesus walks out of Death, he leads the souls of the dead out—the "harrowing of hell." Paul writes: "When he ascended on high he made captivity itself a captive; he gave gifts to his people. When it says, 'He ascended,' what does it mean but that he had also descended into the lower parts of the earth?"[41] The menagerie of the dead to whom Jesus makes this proclamation would include everyone who has died separated from God, including people who haven't even born yet. I know that's a bit of a mind-bender, but when Jesus died he stepped outside of space and time, like everyone who dies. This means his proclamation both has and has not happened at the same time.[42] It is an event that is outside the bounds of time. I realize that many people reading this have heard very little like what I'm suggesting before. However, as I've tried to note, what I'm saying is *not new* within the church. I share the views of many of the earliest pastors and bishops. These views were fairly common—if not dominant—for the first four to five hundred years of church history. Many prevailed well into the fourteenth and fifteenth centuries.

---

41. Ephesians 4:8–9. This is a prime example of a text that causes difficulty in the inerrancy/infallibility debate. I don't believe that hell is in the center of the Earth. That idea is rooted in old theories where people believed in three planes of existence, with a flat Earth at the center of the universe. The biblical writer is accommodating that idea, under inspiration. But that part of the statement is not literally true, it is merely theologically true. Jesus descended into death, but that isn't necessarily a cavern in the middle of the Earth. It is a spiritual plane, more likely a dimension separate from ours outside of space and time as we know it.

42. Think of Schrodinger's cat.

So what happened? Why have the more popular views of *today*: belief in a literal hell in the center of the Earth, where souls of all the lost suffer forever and ever in flames because they didn't invite Jesus into their hearts; a group comprising the vast majority of all people born, who have no hope of changing their destiny after death . . . why have *these* views replaced the ones I shared above? It's a simple question, with an even simpler answer. Can you bring yourself to admit the truth? Pastors and churches embraced *newer* views because they offer religious figures *power*. There is great power in getting to *determine* who is "in" and "out." There is power in being able to create an "other" who we can malign in pious tones and pity. These new views work better at *controlling* people and getting them to offer both obedience and money to the church. Fear sells. Fear raises money. People will willingly cough up cash and follow institutional rules to avoid this kind of "hell." That's what led to the Great Reformation under Luther in 1517—the selling of "indulgences."[43] Today many so-called *Protestants* are preaching the same theology as sixteenth-century Rome, with a different "indulgence." This time it's the "Sinners' Prayer": the magic incantation that keeps you out of eternal torment.

A final word about "heaven." I've said a lot that probably disturbed some people about hell. I've said little about the opposite—heaven. I'm not going to break all this down as I did for hell. I'm just going to put it out there. When Jesus died on the cross, he descended to "the dead." At his resurrection he left the place of the dead with new life. He offered himself as a *ransom* for all people. A price paid to Death[44] to secure the souls of those who had left this life. When he arose he took the dead with him to heaven. His proclamation claimed possession all the souls there—with the theoretical possibility of a *few* hardcore holdouts. "At the name of Jesus every knee should bend, in heaven and on earth and under the earth, and every tongue should confess that Jesus is Lord, to the glory of God the Father."[45] Obeisance *ex post facto*.

43. Basically, "get-out-of-purgatory-free cards," though they weren't exactly "free."

44. Some scholars suggest that Jesus either made his ransom payment to God (PSA), others to the devil (which makes him a near equal to God). I believe this is a *false dichotomy*. If anyone was "paid," it was Death (which doesn't exist ontologically). His payment was made for *our benefit*. The "payment" was solidarity with us in our lifeless condition. The language of "blood" is frequently used in the Bible, because:"The life of the flesh is in the blood; and I have given it to you for making atonement for your lives on the altar; for, as life, it is the blood that makes atonement." Leviticus 17:11.

45. Philippians 2:10–11.

This theological system is built on the understanding that Jesus founded his kingdom two millennia ago. It takes his kingly claims much more literally than modern revivalism. It stresses that Jesus wants people to enjoy his reign in life, and join him in making this world a better place—but it allows him to become Messiah of those who die rejecting him. It is built on the notion that God and Jesus are far more characterized by love and grace than the prevailing belief of most modern evangelicals and fundamentalists today. It may be challenging to many evangelicals, but it is built solidly on Scripture.

10

What Metric Are We Using?

If gold rust, what shall poor iron do?
If a priest is foul, with souls in trust,
Why should a layman curb his lust?
This sight must make the angels weep:
A shepherd shittier than his sheep.
A priest's commitment should be ample
To lead his people by example.

—GEOFFREY CHAUCER[1]

Do not be too quick to condemn the man who no longer believes in God:
for it is perhaps your own coldness and avarice, your mediocrity and materialism,
your sensuality and selfishness that have killed his faith.

—THOMAS MERTON[2]

HOW DO WE MEASURE *"success"* in the church? It's a simple question, but answering it is anything *but* simple! Imagine you've just moved to a new

---

1. Chaucer, *Canterbury Tales*, 33.
2. Merton, *New Seeds of Contemplation*, 177.

community and you're beginning to look for a new church home. What do you do?

Some people consult the yellow pages. They open to the "churches" portion and thumb through looking for the denomination section that interests them. Others might use the "church finder" app on their denominational website, or simply google congregations in the area. Others get recommendations from friends or coworkers. All these approaches reflect normal ways people find information about churches in their area.

After you've formed a list of four, five . . . twelve churches you'll probably take that list and do a "drive-by" next. At this point some very subconscious things begin to happen. You get an initial impression just from a brief glimpse of the building the congregation worships in. Of course, if you've already stalked the church's website (or lack thereof) you're adding this drive-by impression to the feelings you've already begun to form based on *that* exposure. That's why I ask the question: What metric are we using? There are myriad metrics, and most are virtually subconscious to us.

How do we decide which churches are best doing what *Jesus wants*? The Bible doesn't say a lot directly about what a church ought to specifically look like. And there are good reasons for that; that's one of the reasons that the church is so "culturally portable." But that's also one thing that frequently throughout history has been the Achilles' heel of the church—it's so *culturally portable*. We can plant the church in our culture and it will grow. But if it's just growing according to cultural norms it loses much of its power, and can become indistinguishable from the culture around it. Not because it has transformed surrounding culture into the veritable kingdom of God on Earth, but exactly the opposite: the *culture* has morphed the church into a reflection of *itself*. In the first couple chapters I discussed how our pseudo-Christian culture has created certain expectations in belief and practice, right down to politics, and a lot of it isn't remotely Christian. Much of modern American Christianity doesn't look anything like *Jesus*. It could be argued that large swaths of the American church is more American than it is church.

And *our* attitudes often reflect this same cultural influence when we search for a church to identify with. When we do a drive-by we aren't generally asking ourselves if this or that church looks like a good place to *grow as a disciple of Jesus*. Instead, we're more often asking things like: Does it have good "curb appeal"; is it likely to have a good "youth program"; is the music is likely to be what I like; is the parking lot convenient; is it prestigious enough; is it *big* enough? And, sadly, that's what it usually comes down to. It's all just another way of asking: "Is it *American* enough?"

Nearly all Americans are obsessed with size. At this moment Lakewood Church in Houston, Texas, is America's largest congregation. Nearly forty-five thousand people gather each week in the former Compaq Center to "worship." Several million people view these services on TV and online each week. The pastor of this congregation is Joel Osteen. He attended Oral Roberts University, though he didn't graduate. He didn't major in theology, divinity or ministry; he studied television and radio communications. And he is a *wonderful* communicator. His wife, Victoria, is the church's copastor. She attended the University of Houston, where she studied psychology, though she didn't graduate either, and she also lacks formal training in theology. Neither Joel nor Victoria do much that anyone would associate with classical "pastoring." They are more like life coaches or motivational speakers. There's nothing wrong with life coaches or motivational speakers. But those professions serve a function in society that's historically been separate from the sphere of ministers of religion. They aren't the same thing. But forty-five thousand people drive to Lakeside each week to see this new hybrid model. I realize it may sound like I am envious. But I'm not. Really! I actually feel sorry for those who attend the Lakewood *extravaganza*. They're being robbed of the opportunity of being a part of a healthy Christian church. Of course, they are doing this to *themselves*.

The Osteen's have created and marketed their pseudo-religious product very carefully to cash in on America's obsession with superficiality, self-centeredness, and entertainment. They wrap it up with just enough Jesus to make it look religious. They cite just enough Scripture to make it seem holy. And it would appear that they are doing a bang-up job on that front. But I don't regard Lakewood as a successful *congregation*—in fact, I'm not sure I regard it as a church at all. That *may* be going too far, and I readily admit that.

Please hear me: I'm *not* judging Joel, Victoria, or the members of their flock as non-Christians—people who are *going to hell*. I believe they are fellow heirs of the grace of Jesus Christ. I accept them as are my brothers and sisters in the faith. I suspect the Osteens mean well. But they're *not* making *disciples* of Jesus Christ—at least not in any way that reflects two millennia of Christian history. They're doing a uniquely American thing.[3] They are *entertaining* the masses.

---

3. Though this American style religion is now popping up in other places around

Both are very positive and upbeat. They are engaging. They put on a great show. Their message, however, bears little similarity with the message of Jesus. It is conceived of 1970s televangelists and born of Oprah Winfrey. It is positive, self-help, pop psychology. And it's fine as *that*. But it does very little to further the kingdom of Jesus Christ in the world.

Consider the words of Jesus: "If any want to become my followers, let them deny themselves and take up their cross daily and follow me."[4] The message of Joel is decidedly different: "There is a winner in you. You were created to be successful, to accomplish your goals, to leave your mark on this generation. You have greatness in you. The key is to get it out."[5]

Or ponder this saying of Jesus: "My food is to do the will of him who sent me and to complete his work. Do you not say, 'Four months more, then comes the harvest'? But I tell you, look around you, and see how the fields are ripe for harvesting."[6] But according to Osteen: "If you want success, if you want wisdom, if you want to be prosperous and healthy, you're going to have to do more than meditate and believe; you must boldly declare words of faith and victory over yourself and your family."[7] Again, it's *not* that Osteen says anything that is blatantly *heretical*, it's that he's shifted the primary focus *away from the kingdom of God* and placed it on each *individual*. It has pronounced echoes of the old "name it and claim it" theology, without actually crassly saying it. And it subtly transforms the work of the Father from building the kingdom of God on Earth into making each of us affluent and healthy.

In John 16:13–14 Jesus says: "When the Spirit of truth comes, he will guide you into all the truth . . . He will glorify me." Osteen suggests a more egocentric vision for your life: "God would not have put a dream in your heart if He had not already given you everything you need to fulfill it."[8] Instead of glorifying Jesus, the Spirit's job *becomes* planting personal dreams in *your* heart. One of the major snags with this idea is that our dreams are not necessarily divine. In fact, getting our eyes off of ourselves and onto *Jesus' goals* is what *discipleship* is about—it is both a lifelong discipline and an uncommon virtue in American Christianity.

---

the world.

4. Luke 9:23.

5. Osteen, *Daily Readings from You Can, You Will*, 4.

6. John 4:34–36.

7. Osteen, *Your Best Life Now*, 132.

8. Osteen, *Become a Better You*, 9.

Jesus says: "See, I am sending you out like sheep into the midst of wolves; so be wise as serpents and innocent as doves. Beware of them, for they will hand you over to councils and flog you in their synagogues; and you will be dragged before governors and kings because of me, as a testimony to them and the Gentiles . . . you will be hated by all because of my name."[9] Of course, that's not something people want to hear, so Osteen offers a different take: "Start believing today that things are going to change for the better. Your best days are still out in front of you."[10] That's a bit softer on the ear, even if there's no biblical warrant for saying it!

The difference may best be summed up by Mrs. Osteen, whose sermon went viral in 2014. She is seen in the referenced video clip telling congregants at Lakewood:

> I just want to encourage every one of us to realize when we obey God, we're not doing it for God . . . we're doing it for ourselves, because God takes pleasure when we're happy. That's the thing that gives him the greatest joy. So, I want you to know this morning: just do good for your own self. Do good because God wants you to be happy. When you come to church, when you worship him, you're not doing it for God, really. You're doing it for yourself, because that's what makes God happy. Amen?[11]

Joel stands at her side nodding affirmatively and smiling throughout the clip. The scene ends with the congregation applauding enthusiastically. So, the Osteen's suggest, the thing that gives God the greatest joy is when we're happy in this life.

Except. There's. Not. One. Passage. Of. Scripture. That. Says. Anything. Like. That. Not one—not even one that can be ripped out of context to suggest it. *Victoria just made that up out of thin air.* And the crowd went wild! Thousands cheered, and Joel smiled and nodded. But it's just not true. Gone is the idea of taking up a cross to build Christ's kingdom in this fallen world; gone is the Great Commission, where Jesus tells us: "All authority in heaven and on earth has been given to me. Go therefore and make disciples of all nations, baptizing them in the name of the Father and of the Son and of the Holy Spirit, and teaching them to obey everything that I have commanded you."[12] Gone is the teaching that we are members of the body

9. Matthew 10:16–18, 22.

10. Osteen, *Become a Better You*, 375.

11. Osteen, sermon, August 30, 2014.

12. Matthew 28:18–20.

of Christ on Earth, called to combat the forces of evil in high places, as we live differently in this fallen world, following the ethic of the Beatitudes. It's been replaced with *me*, and *my dreams* to prosper in the wealthiest nation the world has ever known. In fact, to the Osteens, God's greatest joy comes from making me happy!

This isn't a benign and insignificant difference. It's vastly at odds with the focus of Christianity in the New Testament. But it's hard to see that in the United States, because it looks just like the native culture of twenty-first-century America. Let's reflect: the eleven apostles[13] all died in service of Christ—ten likely martyred in horrifying ways; Paul was imprisoned countless times, beaten, stoned, and martyred; Jesus' own mom died[14] in relative poverty and obscurity; hundreds of thousands of Christians were killed in the first three centuries of Christianity, just for believing in Jesus. Some were fed to lions in the Coliseum, others immolated to illumine crazy Caesar Nero's garden. But God wants *you* to be happy, suggests Victoria Osteen—*that's* what gives him his greatest joy. Holy narcissism, Batman!

Martin Luther calls this "*Incurvatus in se*"—to be curved inward on oneself. Sorry to be a bubble-buster, but God has a lot bigger things on his mind than your "happiness." Things like: world hunger; out-of-control violence; human trafficking; abuse of the poor; exploitation of women and children around the globe (and closer to home); where that guy who sleeps in the park is going to get his next meal; who's going to notice that Janet at work has a new bruise; and whether the public defender is going to mount an actual defense for sixteen-year-old Tyrrell who did nothing wrong, except look a lot like a *composite* drawing. Avril Lavigne is right: "You can't see the world through a mirror."[15]

We need to "get our heads in the game," move the focus off of ourselves, and begin to work as God's hands and feet in the world, making a positive difference. We need to be active participants in building God's kingdom of justice and equity for all people. We do that building by seeking "righteousness." Biblical righteousness is much more concerned about the rights and dignity of the poor and marginalized than picking and choosing Old Testament civil or ceremonial laws to compel others to keep. Righteousness isn't even about personal morality. It's about *social justice.* Consider

13. Minus Judas.

14. Some Christian traditions contend that Mary was assumed directly into heaven without first dying. Most teach that she died and was buried like all other humans.

15. Lavigne, "Too Much to Ask."

Ezekiel 18:5–9: "A man is righteous and does what is lawful and right—if he does not . . . oppress anyone, but restores to the debtor his pledge, commits no robbery, gives his bread to the hungry and covers the naked with a garment, does not take advance or accrued interest, withholds his hand from iniquity, executes true justice between contending parties, follows my statutes, and is careful to observe my ordinances, acting faithfully—such a one is righteous."[16]

And that's the major failing of big churches. They make it easy for anyone to sit in the crowd and remain *passive*. They (inadvertently) create a multitude of *spectators* with few participants. Their emphasis on "excellence" only makes this worse. Jesus frequently sent his disciples out and expected them to fall short, get confused, and even fail. He then discusses the disconnect between their beliefs and their actions. His followers grow as *disciples* through their failures, because he coached them. We all understand that people learn much more by doing than by sitting around and listening to someone talk about something. Large congregations limit that experience. Jesus was always much more interested in being truly involved in the whole lives of his small band of disciples. He loved the masses, but he said and did things to keep them at arm's length.[17] He *pastored* the 70, or 120-ish.

Large churches virtually *compel* people to assume a spectator role, relegating people into anonymous "faces in the crowd." And that's the other cutting edge of the sword—there is little, if any, accountability in a megachurch. For this reason they are less challenging. This is not how the church has operated throughout history. Christianity has always been nurtured and expressed in smallish communities, at least until recently. And the megachurch model isn't creating healthy Christians. It generally isn't even trying to do that. Most of the people who assemble at large churches are there precisely because they desire to *watch* a great *spectacle* of preaching and musical performance as anonymous consumers religious goods and services. It's creating customers focused on themselves—the exact opposite of what discipleship is. *Incurvatus in se* flawlessly presented to sooth our American anxieties. And the echoes reverberate all through the church in America—big and small![18]

---

16. Also see Isaiah 58:6–14 and Micah 6:8.

17. See the second half of John 6, after the feeding of the five thousand. Jesus even asks if his hard words offended the masses (as he seems to have intended).

18. The median attendance of an American church is seventy people, the average size

We need to ask ourselves if the metric we use to evaluate congregational "success" is biblical. The Bible seems disinterested in *size* as a number of consequence. The scriptural directive is to make disciples—people who fashion their whole way of life after Jesus'. This alone is the metric that Jesus uses. We need to make it ours!

is four hundred (a number skewed greatly by the forty largest congregations, whose attendance is over ten thousand each). See Chaves and Eagle, "Religious Congregations in 21st Century America," 5.

11

A Simple Question

There are two kinds of people:
those who say to God, "Thy will be done," and
those to whom God says, "All right, then, have it your way."

—C. S. Lewis[1]

Nothing profits more
Than self-esteem, grounded on what is just and right.

—John Milton[2]

What do you want from Jesus? What you come to the Messiah for will dictate, to a large extent, what your spiritual life will look like. Consider motivation of the five thousand:

> Jesus said, "Make the people sit down." Now there was a great deal of grass in the place; so they sat down, about five thousand in all. Then Jesus took the loaves, and when he had given thanks, he distributed them to those who were seated; so also the fish, as much as they wanted. When they were satisfied, he told his disciples, "Gather up the fragments left over, so that nothing may be lost."

1. Lewis, *Great Divorce*, 72.
2. Milton, "Paradise Lost," 513.

So they gathered them up, and from the fragments of the five barley loaves, left by those who had eaten, they filled twelve baskets. When the people saw the sign that he had done, they began to say, "This is indeed the prophet who is to come into the world." When Jesus realized that they were about to come and take him by force to make him king, he withdrew again to the mountain by himself.[3]

Now ponder the needs expressed by the Syrophoenician woman:

From there he set out and went away to the region of Tyre. He entered a house and did not want anyone to know he was there. Yet he could not escape notice, but a woman whose little daughter had an unclean spirit immediately heard about him, and she came and bowed down at his feet. Now the woman was a Gentile, of Syrophoenician origin. She begged him to cast the demon out of her daughter. He said to her, "Let the children be fed first, for it is not fair to take the children's food and throw it to the dogs." But she answered him, "Sir, even the dogs under the table eat the children's crumbs." Then he said to her, "For saying that, you may go—the demon has left your daughter." So she went home, found the child lying on the bed, and the demon gone.[4]

What did the people in these two accounts want from Jesus? You may be tempted to say, "miracles." And that's technically correct; but that's only half the story. In the first account five thousand Jewish men sought to make Jesus their king. They were planning to seize him and *compel* him to accept that role. But his kingship would have been defined by satisfying the expectations of those who anointed him. He would be a "king" only to the extent that he acted the part of a genie. The people would have been the ones holding the reins. Many Christians today want exactly this kind of God. They want Jesus as long as he makes their lives easier in some way: curing their loved ones from cancer; getting them promotions and raises; keeping their children safe; making them feel "saved," forgiven, righteous, and full of joy; making their spouse do *whatever* they think "good Christian spouses" do; or whatever their particular desire happens to be. As long as Jesus helps accomplish that, they'll "faithfully follow."

Theologians call this the "theology of glory." Most *immature* Christians embrace this style of theology, and that's to be expected as long as it's a *phase* we pass *through* on our way to *adulthood*. It's like adolescence. And

3. John 6:10–15.
4. Mark 7:24–30.

every parent I know (including myself) breathes a giant sigh of relief as their kids begin showing signs of maturing *out* of adolescence. If a person stops developing at this self-centered phase, there's a problem!

Unfortunately this is exactly what has happened *spiritually* to far too many American Christians. Many are rarely encouraged to push/grow deeper in their faith than their own egocentricity. Their religious development remains stunted as a result. And many of their pastors are afraid to lead them to greater maturity because they fear being fired for failing to meet the expectations of the flock they're supposed to *lead*. Many also fear significant numbers of their congregation will *flee* this kind of preaching in favor of the easy-listening sermons down the street. And these fears are *justified*! A lot of Christians do just that! Many people "church shop" until they find cozy congregations in which to be entertained and amused.

A seminal passage forming the identity of the people of God in the Old Testament is found in Genesis 32:22–32:

> The same night [Jacob] got up and took his two wives, his two maids, and his eleven children, and crossed the ford of the Jabbok. He took them and sent them across the stream, and likewise everything that he had. Jacob was left alone; and a man wrestled with him until daybreak. When the man saw that he did not prevail against Jacob, he struck him on the hip socket; and Jacob's hip was put out of joint as he wrestled with him. Then he said, "Let me go, for the day is breaking." But Jacob said, "I will not let you go, unless you bless me." So he said to him, "What is your name?" And he said, "Jacob." Then the man said, "You shall no longer be called Jacob, but Israel, for you have striven with God and with humans, and have prevailed." Then Jacob asked him, "Please tell me your name?" But he said, "Why is it that you ask my name?" And there he blessed him. So Jacob called the place Peniel, saying, "For I have seen God face to face, and yet my life is preserved." The sun rose upon him as he passed Penuel, limping because of his hip. Therefore to this day the Israelites do not eat the thigh muscle that is on the hip socket, because he struck Jacob on the hip socket at the thigh muscle.

There are many things going on in this passage. But one of the most important is the fact that Jacob wrestles with God, and *God hurts Jacob in the process*—badly. Paul tells the Christians at Galatia that Old Testament spirituality served as our "schoolmaster."[5] If this is true, Christianity

---

5. Galatians 3:24–26.

shouldn't view itself as exempt from wrestling with God. If anything, we ought to be wrestling with him *more*. That's our *spiritual heritage*. Moving from the "nursery" (to use Paul's metaphor) into adulthood should cause us to expect more *painful* encounters with God, not fewer! A faith that wrestles with God has scars. These aren't marks of failure; they show where we have been "pruned" by a master "vinedresser" (to use another common scriptural metaphor). Such events in our lives should cause us to ascribe glory to God for who he *is*, not for what *goodies* he provides.

The expectations of the Syrophoenician woman differ greatly from those of the five thousand. If you read just a few verses past the miraculous multiplication of the bread and fish, you'll see that Jesus told these Jews: "Unless you eat the flesh of the Son of Man and drink his blood, you have no life in you. Those who eat my flesh and drink my blood have eternal life, and I will raise them up on the last day; for my flesh is true food and my blood is true drink. Those who eat my flesh and drink my blood abide in me, and I in them."[6] It can't be overstated how *objectionable* this imagery was to Jewish people. The Law required Israelites to eat no meat with blood in it—it had to be cooked to well-done. (Which should be a crime, but it was their reality.) Even touching blood, or sitting in a chair a menstruating woman had sat in, made a one "unclean."[7] So this discourse could only have one outcome—*offense*. But that *offense* is a starting point for *something else*. Those who stuck with Jesus after this sermon were at a point in their maturity where they could move deeper. Sadly, most of the five thousand were not at that point. But for those who were he was able to begin to move them beyond Old Testament prescriptions and prohibitions and into the New Testament ethic of sacrificial love.

Jesus offers a similar offense to the Syrophoenician mother—he calls her a "dog."[8] It would have been easy for her to take up that obvious offense, snort, and walk away like most of the five thousand did. But she didn't. And a big part of why she didn't is what she *sought* from Jesus. She didn't want just any old miracle, like a religious high or bread for one meal. She wanted what only God could give—*deliverance from Satan*. No matter what you and I may think of demon possession, in the New Testament the idea of demonic possession is presented repeatedly as an experience that was

6. John 6:53–57.

7. Leviticus 15:19–20.

8. Some might argue that he merely implied it, but the implication is quite clear. We can't let Jesus off the hook; he did it, and he meant to do it.

both evil and destructive to humans. It was something over which there was no human control. The Syrophoenician woman says her daughter was possessed of evil spirits, and there was no human hope for her. This drove her to Jesus. She doesn't see him as some great human doctor, or life coach. She sees him as the instrument of God. He was her only hope. Jesus could work with that!

Metaphorically, our whole world is presented by Scripture as being enslaved to Satan. Its innate values are often self-centered and corrupt. Its enticements are myriad and frequently lead to entrapment and death. Solutions to problems in the world typically drip with the blood of violence. Are we seeking a deliverance from life in this world that can only come from the Son of God? Or are we seeking something far less extraordinary from our Lord?

There is nothing wrong with being concerned with temporal and physical things. "Daily bread" is a central part of the Lord's Prayer. But it is not the *only* part, and it isn't the most important part. In fact Jesus tells us: "When you are praying, do not heap up empty phrases as the Gentiles do; for they think that they will be heard because of their many words. Do not be like them, for your Father knows what you need before you ask him."[9] We don't need to beg for God to take an interest in our physical needs. He is already both keenly aware of them, and positively disposed to help us as will be best for us. That doesn't mean that he'll always do what we want. But it does mean God is paying attention, and that he's aware of our needs.

The activity of prayer is more for our benefit than it is for God; the same is true of worship. God doesn't need us to pray to inform him of our needs. God doesn't need us to worship him to salve his voracious ego. Prayer and worship are designed to help *us* articulate our needs, and place them *into* God's hands. This aids us in moving beyond things which are easily seen, toward a mental state that views this world differently. Worship prompts us to speak our veneration of someone *greater* than ourselves, and allegiance to a kingdom beyond default human greed. Prayer and worship get us *out of ourselves* and mitigate *incurvatus in se*.[10] These two disciplines help fix our gaze on the divine in ways that help us to see other people as our equals, moving us *beyond* our ourselves, our "clan," and our nation, and *into* beholding all other humans as fellow children of God. That's what's

---

9. Matthew 6:7–8.

10. Being curved inward on oneself.

going on for the Twelve and the other Jews who witnessed Jesus' interaction with the Syrophoenician woman.

Many of the people who first read the Gospels had experienced real persecution. It would have been easy for them to allow fear to dominate their lives. That, in turn, could have caused them to hide their faith from people who were different from them. They could have withdrawn into secretive enclaves that shunned outsiders. Their struggles weren't about trivial matters like youth programming or a preferred musical genre. They didn't go to church as consumers of religious entertainment, to watch their pastor rappel into the auditorium from the ceiling, or be entertained by a top-notch rock band for seventy-five minutes. They weren't looking to "feel close to Jesus" as if he was their *boyfriend*. They went to the gathering of the *ecclesia*[11] to hear the kingdom of God *announced* as a *present real-ity*, of which they were a vital part. They went to encounter Jesus, not just *subjectively* in their heart, but *objectively* in the Eucharist, and within the community of people who comprised the body of Christ in their locale. It was a place where they gathered in solidarity with other followers of Jesus: fellow members of his kingdom, no matter how different from one another.

They assembled to be reminded that they had been ransomed by Jesus out of bondage to the world's fallenness and transferred into the kingdom Jesus established in his first advent: "He has rescued us from the power of darkness and transferred us into the kingdom of his beloved Son, in whom we have redemption, the forgiveness of sins."[12] For early Christians the church was the place where our inheritance was glimpsed, where partakers shared this gift with one another. The Syrophoenician woman serves as a surrogate for all who feel estranged from God and his people. She is *heroic* because in the face of offense and dismissiveness, she stands firm and accepts insult. She does it while holding onto her trust in Jesus as her solution. She is a marvelous example of Christian discipleship. She bows before the Son of God and seeks the "salvation" of *another*. She enlists Christ's aid in divine warfare against the threefold enemy of humanity: sin, death, and the devil. She does this while being insulted by God himself.

11. The Greek word translated as "church," which is the same word used centuries before to denote the main democratic assembly of ancient Athens. It was the special group that had voice in ruling that premiere Greek city-state. The special task of these men (they were always highborn males) was to serve the interests of the "lower" classes, and all of Greek society.

12. Colossians 1:13–14; see also Ephesians 1:11–14.

So, what do you seek from God? And how much are you willing to *give* to get it? If you're seeking mostly human things from Jesus—some sort of vague happy feeling, an elevated moral ethic, good social connections, prestige, wealth, well-behaved children, self-satisfaction, a divine diet plan, an improved sex life,[13] a religious "high" of some sort, or some other fleshly desire—when God insults your religious sensibilities you're going to have a mighty crisis on your hands. And he will do that; I guarantee it! Jesus is looking for people who are actually followers—people who are willing to work to *model* their whole lives around him. Christianity isn't just: an intellectual calling, where God gets us to believe right things about him; nor is it a moral calling, where he tells us to avoid certain sins; and it's not primarily an altruistic calling, where Jesus turns us into "do-gooders." It's all three *and a lot more.* Jesus wants our heads, our hearts, and our hands. He wants them even when everything is going to hell around us. He wants them *especially* when everything is going to hell around us. He doesn't want them casually, until we get what *we want from him,* only to wander off again and return to business as usual.[14] He wants us to incarnate his kingdom reality in the world around us, and to sacrifice of ourselves to draw others into the enterprise.

We do that by embracing the Beatitudes within our faith communities, and taking up our calling as ambassadors of reconciliation.[15] That role is expressed through grace and mercy, not law. James makes this very clear for us: "Mercy triumphs over judgment."[16] Judgment and threats of condemnation are the main tools of Satan; they are how he keeps people trapped (in their own minds, at least) in sin and death. Christ triumphed over these and crushed the head of Satan as he arose on the first Easter morning.

So, what are you seeking from Jesus? Is it primarily about *you*? Or are you engaged in following him and making the *world* a better place? Even if it's only a very little piece of it wherever you live. Are you mostly seeking a warm, fuzzy feeling in this life, and an eternal dwelling in the next.[17] Or are you willing to put those things on the "back burner," while

---

13. Over the past several years literally hundreds of churches have titillated their communities with sermon series on spicing up your marriage with biblical how-to sermons on sex. Seriously.

14. A cycle we see play out all through the pages of the Old Testament.

15. 2 Corinthians 5.

16. James 2:13.

17. "Getting saved" to go to heaven and avoid hell is often referred to as "fire insurance."

you build Christ's kingdom here and now for others—even "dogs" who we aren't fond of? And will you do it even when *God* hurts you? Jesus does promise "heaven" to his followers, but he spends far more time urging us to live differently in the here and now. He urges us to be his representatives in our small corner of the world, and simply trust that he is good for the other things because he promised them.

What you're seeking determines your focus. If you're thinking primarily of yourself, that's a problem, at least to Jesus! He calls us to be focused on *his kingdom*. And this is the difference between "spiritual" and "religious." Both are important, but one is more importanter[18] and feeds the other. We all know the popular American sentiment, "I'm spiritual, not religious." And that idea lies at the heart of our culture's problem. We have it backwards.

I get why people sometimes want to distance themselves from "organized religion," "the institutional church," and "religion." These things have failed us often enough. They're often biased, bigoted, and boorish—at least in their public persona. As a minister I often feel the same way. Part of why I've written this is to provide a contrary view to the dominant evangelical/ fundamentalist expression of Christianity within our country. I've done it because they embarrass me and frustrate me with their legalism, narrow-mindedness, and anti-intellectualism.

But citing the obvious flaws of the church as an excuse to "check out" is a cop out. All institutions fail us, because all institutions are comprised of people. And people are flawed. Some very deeply. Baseball and football have been wracked with public scandals in recent years, but few suggest they're giving up the NFL because of them.[19] Hollywood is proving to be a seriously flawed institution, especially toward women. Yet many television shows and movies produced today are serious works of art and intellect. They have much to teach us. Even as they have much work to do to make their institution better.

People will always fail us—including *ourselves*. But I've never yet heard someone suggest they are giving up their *private* faith because they've discovered *they're* a creep. Let's be honest: scandals have happened within the church, but most people are quitting religion because it requires *effort*, not because they've been personally harmed by a flawed religious leader.

---

18. I know!

19. I say this as a fan of the Chicago Bears, so trust me when I say that I fully understand the temptation to bail on organizations that fail their supporters by making bad decision after bad decision.

They drop out (or fail to join in) because they'd prefer not to be a part of the solution—it requires more than they're willing to give. Their focus is *incurvatus in se*. "Spirituality" can only develop in *healthy ways* as a part of a group—in a "religion"—where others can hold us accountable to our own *selfishnesses* (which are generally invisible to us). Engaging in service to others is what best pulls us out of our inward bent and enables us to become actualized people. Personal "spirituality" has done very little to make the world a better place; but "religion," groups of congregations working together for a common principle, has done a great deal to provide progress for humanity. That's not to suggest that religion hasn't done harm at times. It has. But those moments are the exception, not the rule. And a healthier, moderate or progressive branch of religion could have stopped most of the worst of those.[20]

That's my other reason for writing this book. The apparent ascendancy of very "conservative" (or regressive) modes of Christianity, mixed with anti-intellectualism and an emphasis on personal salvation (as opposed to a focus on community), is bringing us to dangerous moment. There are numerous politicians and religious leaders who have openly announced their plans to infiltrate America's government to accomplish a *coup d'état* "for Jesus." Roy Moore showed us how close our society is to tipping in the wrong direction. They don't care that Jesus expressly stated: "My kingdom is not from this world."[21] They don't seem to understand what he meant when he said: "The kingdom of God is not coming with things that can be observed; nor will they say, 'Look, here it is!' or 'There it is!' For, in fact, the kingdom of God is among you."[22] Christ has called us to do it by living the Beatitudes in our world, living with values rooted in God and in the universal brotherhood of humanity. Despite these passages, they desire to create a theocracy, with *themselves* in positions of power over the rest of us. We'll never be free of those whose aspiration to enslave us in religious fundamentalism—they always exist, in every culture and in every religious expression. However, it is not enough for ministers to stand in contradistinction to these who preach zealotry. We need whole *congregations* working together to incarnate a different reality. We need a lot of them.

20. It is almost always the hyper-conservative branches of religions that do the greatest harm in the name of God, like the Crusades, Spanish Inquisition, Puritans, KKK, and ISIL.

21. John 18:36

22. Luke 17:20–21.

His call goes back to the creation myth, where we see God as creator of the universe and of humanity. We see Cain and Abel—brothers who are different in myriad ways—yet both loved by God. God wishes to approve both, but one is unwilling to submit to "institutional religion." He breaks from worshipping God in the prescribed way, and in a jealous rage kills the one who was. God asks Cain the question that has haunted people ever since: "Where is your brother?" God forces Cain to confront his actions and give an account. But Cain tries to shrug off that responsibility, as so many do today: "I don't know, am I my brother's keeper?"[23] The implied answer is: "Yes, yes you are!"

How are we doing at that?

The original question in this chapter was, "What do you want from Jesus?" That answer is tied up with the answer to this question. We need divine help in getting past our selfish bent. If you're not seeking that, you are still living in the clutches of this world's system. God promises in Genesis 4:7: "If you do well, will you not be accepted? And if you do not do well, sin is lurking at the door; its desire is for you, but you must master it." May we answer loud and clear with our lives. And may God richly bless you as you struggle like Jacob/Israel to follow Jesus the Christ in your everyday life.

23. Genesis 4:8.

Bibliography

Al-Zarqawi, Abu Musab. "Katrina an Answer to Prayers." *World*, September 11, 2005, http://www.cnn.com/2005/WORLD/meast/09/11/zarqawi.message/

Alighieri, Dante. *Inferno*. Translated by Courtney Langdon. Cambridge, MA: Harvard University Press, 1918.

Asimov, Isaac. "A Cult of Ignorance." *Newsweek* 95/3 (January 21, 1980) 19.

Atwood, Margaret. *The Handmaid's Tale*. New York: Houghton Mifflin Harcourt, 1986.

Aulén, Gustaf. *Christus Victor: An Historical Study of the Three Main Types of the Idea of the Atonement*. New York: MacMillan, 1960.

Bailey, Philip James. *Festus*. London: Pickering, 1839.

Bell, Rob. *Love Wins: A Book about Heaven, Hell, and the Fate of Every Person Who Ever Lived*. New York: HarperOne, 2011.

Bolz-Webber, Nadia. *Pastorix*. New York: Jericho, 2013.

Bonheoffer, Dietrich. *The Cost of Discipleship*. New York: MacMillan, 1979.

Borg, Marcus. *Reading the Bible Again for the First Time: Taking the Bible Seriously but Not Literally*. San Francisco: HarperSanFrancisco, 2001.

Boyd, Gregory A. *Crucifixion of the Warrior God: Interpreting the Old Testament's Violent Portraits of God in Light of the Cross*. 2 vols. Minneapolis: Fortress, 2017.

Brueggemann, Walter. *Sabbath as Resistance: Saying No to the Culture of Now*. Louisville: Westminster John Knox, 2014.

Burton, Tara. "Major Evangelical Leader Says Trump Gets a 'Mulligan' on Stormy Daniels Affair." *Vox*, January 23, 2018. https://www.vox.com/identities/2018/1/23/16924546/evangelical-tony-perkins-trump-stormy-daniels-affair-mulligan.

Cass, Gary. "Why I'm Absolutely Islamophobic." *Charisma*, September 3, 2014. http://defendchristians.org/ commentary/im-islamaphobic-are-you/.

Chaucer, Geoffrey. *The Canterbury Tales: In Modern Verse*. Translated by Joseph Glaser. Indianapolis: Hackett, 2005.

Chaves, Mark, and Alison Eagle. "Religious Congregations in 21st Century America." *National Congregations Study*. Durham, NC: Duke University, 2012. http://www.soc.duke.edu/natcong/Docs/NCSIII_report_final.pdf.

Chesterton, G. K. *Tremendous Trifles*. New York: Dodd & Mead, 1910.

Clark, Chap. *Hurt: Inside the World of Today's Teenagers*. Grand Rapids: Baker Academic, 2004.

commings, e.e. "since feeling is first." *Is 5*. New York: Liveright, 1985.

Cox, Harvey. *The Secular City*. New York: Collier, 1965.

Crane, Stephen. *The Red Badge of Courage.* Kolkata, India: Signet, 2011.

Criminal Minds. "Seven Seconds." Season 3, episode 5. Written by Andi Bushell. Directed by John Gallagher. CBS. October 24, 2007.

Crossan, Dominic. *Who Is Jesus?: Answers to Your Questions about the Historical Jesus.* Westminster: John Knox, 1999.

Dead Poet's Society. Directed by Peter Weir. Film. Hollywood: Touchstone Pictures, 1989.

Dear, John. *Put Down Your Sword: Answering the Gospel Call to Creative Nonviolence.* Grand Rapids: Eerdmans, 2008.

Dickinson, Emily. "Tell All the Truth." Poem #1129. *Wikisource.* https://en.wikisource. org/ wiki/Tell_all_the_Truth_but_tell_it_slant_.

Dixon, A. C., and R. A. Torrey. *The Fundamentals: A Testimony to the Truth.* Los Angeles: Bible Institute of Los Angels, 1917.

Douthat, Ross. *Bad Religion: How We Became a Nation of Heretics.* New York: Free Press, 2012.

Dyson, Michael. *Come Hell or High Water.* Cambridge: Civitas, 2006.

Eagleton, Terry. *On Evil.* New Haven, CT: Yale Press, 2010.

Edwards, Jonathan. "Sinners in the Hands of an Angry God." Boston: Kneeland & Green, July 8, 1741.

Eliot, T. S. *The Cocktail Party.* New York: Harcourt & Brace, 1950.

Ellul, Jacques. *The Meaning of the City.* Translated by Dennis Pardee. Grand Rapids: Eerdmans, 1970.

———. *Violence: Reflections from a Christian Perspective.* Translated by Cecelia Gaul Kings. New York: Seabury, 1969.

Enns, Peter. *The Bible Tells Me So: Why Defending Scripture Has Made Us Unable to Read It.* New York: HarperOne, 2014.

———. *The Evolution of Adam: What the Bible Does and Doesn't Say about Human Origins.* Grand Rapids: Brazos, 2012.

Evans, Rachel Held. "Why Progressive Christians Should Care about Abortion." Blog post, May 2, 2013. http://rachelheldevans.com/blog/why-progressive-christians-should-care-about-abortion-gosnell.

Flynn, Robert. *Lawful Abuse: How the Century of the Child became the Century of the Corporation.* San Antonio: Wings, 2012.

Foerst, Anna. *God in the Machine: What Robots Teach Us about Humanity and God.* New York: Dutton, 2004.

Gagnon, Robert A. J. *The Bible and Homosexual Practice: Texts and Hermeneutics.* Nashville: Abingdon, 2002.

Gaiman, Neil. *Coraline.* New York: Harper Collins, 2002.

Geisler, Norman. *Ethics: Alternatives and Issues.* Grand Rapids: Zondervan, 1971.

Gibbs, Eddie. *ChurchNext: Quantum Changes in How We Do Ministry.* Downers Grove, IL: InterVarsity, 2000.

Hawkins, Kristin. Interview on *The Joy Reid Show.* MSNBC, January 28, 2017. https://www.rawstory.com/ 2017/01/anti-choice-advocate-admits-to-joy-reid-her-ultimate-goal-is-to-make-birth-control-illegal/.

Hedges, Chris. *American Fascists: The Christian Right and the War on America.* New York: Free Press, 2006.

Henderson, David W. *Culture Shift: Communicating God's Truth to Our Changing World.* Grand Rapids: Baker,1998.

Idol, Billy. *White Wedding.* Single LP. London: Chrysalis, June 21, 1982.

International Council on Biblical Inerrancy. "The Chicago Statement on Biblical Inerrancy." Matthews, NC: Bastion, October 28, 1978.

Jerman, Jenna, Rachel K. Jones, and Tsuyoshi Onda. "Characteristics of US Abortion Patients in 2014 and Changes since 2008." *Guttmacher Institute Report*, May, 2016. https://www.guttmacher.org/ report/characteristics-us-abortion-patients-2014.

Jewel. "Hands." *Spirit*. Musical album. New York: Atlantic, November 17, 1998.

Keller, Timothy. *The Prodigal God: Recovering the Heart of the Christian Faith*. New York: Penguin, 2008.

Kimball, Dan. *They Like Jesus but Not the Church*. Grand Rapids: Zondervan, 2007.

King, Martin Luther, Jr. *Where Do We Go from Here: Chaos or Community*. Boston: Beacon. 1967.

Kinnaman, David. *Unchristian: What a New Generation Really Thinks about Christianity . . . and Why It Matters*. Grand Rapids: Baker, 2007.

LaHaye, Tim, and Jerry Jenkins. *Left Behind*. 16 vols. Carol Stream: Tyndale, 2008.

Lavigne, Avril "Too Much to Ask." *Let Go*. Musical lbum. New York: Arista, June 4, 2002.

Lewis, C. S. *The Great Divorce*. Nashville: Broadman & Holman, 1996.

Lincoln, Abraham. "The Gettysburg Address." November 19, 1863.

Lindsey, Hal. *The Late Great Planet Earth*. Grand Rapids: Zondervan, 1970.

Luther, Martin. *The Small Catechism*. Saint Louis: Concordia, 2005.

McGrath, Alister. *Heresy: A History of Defending the Faith*. New York: HarperOne, 2009.

McGrath, James F. "Swing By and Pick Up the Llamas." *Patheos*, February 22, 2016. http:// www.patheos.com/ blogs/religionprof/2016/02/swing-by-and-pick-up-the-llamas. html.

McKinley, Rick. *Jesus in the Margins*. Sisters, OR: Multnomah, 2005.

McKnight, Scot. *The Jesus Creed: Loving God, Loving Others*. Brewster, MA: Paraclete, 2004.

McLaren, Brian. *A Generous Orthodoxy*. Grand Rapids: Zondervan, 2004.

———. *A New Kind of Christianity*. New York: HarperOne, 2010.

———. *Why Did Jesus, Moses, the Buddha, and Mohammed Cross the Road: Christian Identity in a Multi-Faith World*. New York: Jericho, 2012.

McNeal, Reggie. *The Present Future: Six Tough Questions for the Church*. San Francisco: Jossy-Bass, 2003.

Merton, Thomas. *New Seeds of Contemplation*. New York: New Directions, 1961.

Milton, John. "Paradise Lost." In *The Complete Poetical Works of John Milton*. New York: Modern Library, 2007.

Moltmann, Jürgen. *The Crucified God: The Cross of Christ as the Foundation and Criticism of Christian Theology*. New York: Harper & Row, 1974.

Moon, Ruth. "Does Plan B Cause Abortion?" *Christianity Today*, April 5, 2013. http:// www.christianitytoday.com/ct/2013/may/does-plan-b-cause-abortion.html.

Newbigin, Lesslie. *The Gospel in a Pluralist Society*. Grand Rapids: Eerdmans, 1989.

Niebuhr, H. Richard. *Christ and Culture*. New York: Harper & Row, 1951.

Nietzsche, Friedrich. *Beyond Good and Evil*. Translated by Helen Zimmern. Norwalk: Easton, 1994.

Noll, Mark A. *The Scandal of the Evangelical Mind*. Grand Rapids: Eerdmans, 1994.

Osteen, Joel. *Become a Better You*. New York: Free Press, 2007.

———. *Daily Readings from You Can, You Will: 90 Devotions to Becoming a Winner*. New York: FaithWords, 2015.

————. *Your Best Life Now: 7 Steps to Living at Your Full Potential*. New York: FaithWords, 2014.

Osteen, Victoria. Sermon, August 30, 2014. https://www.youtube.com/watch?v=hbZHgGMe31s.

Plato. "Symposium." In *Selected Writings on Socrates, Plato, Aristophanes, Xenophon*. London: Collectors, 2004.

Robertson, Pat. *The 700 Club*, September 12, 2005.

Robinson, John A. T. *Honest to God*. Philadelphia: Westminster, 1963.

Rohr, Richard. "A Toxic Image of God." Center for Action and Contemplation, January 28, 2016. https://cac.org/a-toxic-image-of-god-2016-11-28/

Santorum, Rick. Speech. C-SPAN, February 27, 2015. https://www.c-span.org/video/?324558-13/rick-santorum-remarks-cpac.

Schneible, Ann. "Pope Francis: Fear and Joylessness Are Signs of Bad Spiritual Health." *EWTN News*, May 15, 2015. http://ewtnnews.com/catholic-news/Vatican.php?id=12085.

Shakespeare, William. *Hamlet, Prince of Denmark*. Roslyn, NY: Walter J. Black, 1937.

Smith, Gregory, Jessica Martinez. "How the Faithful Voted: A Preliminary 2016 Analysis." *Facttank: News in the Numbers*, November 9, 2016. http://www.pewresearch.org/fact-tank/2016/11/09/how-the-faithful-voted-a-preliminary-2016-analysis/.

Spong, John. *Biblical Literalism: A Gentile Heresy*. New York: HarperOne, 2017.

Stripe, Claude, et al. "A Protestant Affirmation on the Control of Human Reproduction." *Journal of the American Scientific Affiliation* 23/2 (June, 1970) 46–47.

Sun Tzu. *On the Art of War*. Translated by Lionel Giles. New York: Routledge, 2013.

Sweeney, Jon M. *Inventing Hell: Dante, the Bible, and Eternal Torment*. New York: Jericho, 2014.

Taylor, Daniel. *The Myth of Certainty: The Reflective Christian and the Risk of Commitment*. Downers Grove, IL: InterVarsity, 1986.

Thielicke, Helmut. *Between Heaven and Earth: Conversations with American Christians*. New York: Harper & Row, 1965.

————. *Our Heavenly Father*. Trans. John W. Doberstein. New York: Harper & Row, 1960.

Thompson, Peter, producer. "Global Wildlife Populations Have Fallen by Half—a Stat That Says It All." *The World*, October 1, 2014. https://www.pri.org/stories/2014-10-01/global-wildlife-populations-have-fallen-half-stat-says-it-all.

Thoreau, Henry David. *Walden*. New York: Longmans & Green, 1910.

Tickle, Phyllis. *The Great Emergence: How Christianity Is Changing and Why*. Grand Rapids: Baker, 2008.

Tillich, Paul. *The Eternal Now*. New York: Scribner's, 1956.

————. *The New Being*. New York: Scribner's, 1955.

Vines, Matthew. *God and the Gay Christian*. New York: Convergent, 2014.

Walsh, Matt. "Attention, Pro-Aborts: Here Are Two Arguments You Can't Make Anymore." *TheBlaze*, July 15, 2015. https://www.theblaze.com/contributions/attention-pro-aborts-here-are-two-arguments-you-cant-make-anymore.

Waltke, Bruce. "Contraception and Abortion." *Christianity Today* 13/3 (November 5, 1968) 3.

Ware, Kallistos. *The Orthodox Way*. Crestwood, NY: St. Vladimir's Seminary Press, 1979.

Webb, Jimmy. *Would You Like to Ride in My Beautiful Balloon?* Musical album performed by The Fifth Dimension. Detroit: Soul City, March 11, 1967.

Webber, Robert. *Ancient-Future Faith: Rethinking Evangelicalism for a Postmodern World.* Grand Rapids: Baker, 1999.

Wingren, Gustaf. *Luther on Vocation.* Edinburgh: Oliver & Boyd, 1958.

Wood, Gabby. "Neil Gaiman on the Meaning of Fairy Tales." *The Telegraph*, November 20, 2014. http://www.telegraph.co.uk/culture/books/11243761/Neil-Gaiman-Disneys-Sleeping-Beauty.html.

Woolf, Virginia. *Between the Acts.* London: Hogarth, 1941.

Wright, N. T. *Evil and the Justice of God.* Downers Grove, IL: InterVarsity, 2006.

———. *How God Became King: The Forgotten Story of the Gospels.* New York: HarperOne, 2012.

———. *Justification.* Downers Grove, IL: IVP Academic, 2009.

Yaconelli, Michael. *Messy Spirituality.* Grand Rapids: Zondervan, 2002.

Zizioulas, John D. *Being as Communion.* Crestwood, NY: St. Vladimir's Seminary Press, 1997.

Made in the USA
Middletown, DE
05 October 2018